TEACHER'S PET PUBLICATIONS

PUZZLE PACK
for
Macbeth

based on the play by
William Shakespeare

Written by
William T. Collins

© 2005 Teacher's Pet Publications
All Rights Reserved

The materials in this packet are copyrighted
by Teacher's Pet Publications, Inc.

These pages may be duplicated by the purchaser
for use in the purchaser's own classroom.

Copying any of these materials and distributing them
for any other purpose is a violation of the copyright laws.

© 2005 Teacher's Pet Publications, Inc.
www.tpet.com

INTRODUCTION
If you already own the LitPlan for this title, this Puzzle Pack will refresh your Unit Resource Materials and Vocabulary Resource Materials sections plus give you additional materials you can substitute into the tests. If you do not already have a complete LitPlan, these pages will give you some supplemental materials to use with your own plan. There are two main groups of materials: one set for unit words (such as characters' names, symbols, places, etc.) and one set for vocabulary words associated with the book.

WORD LIST
There is a word list for both the unit words and the vocabulary words. These lists show you which words are being used in the materials and the clues or definitions being used for those words. You may want to give students a word list with clues/definitions to help them, or you may want students to only have a word list (without clues/definitions) if you want them to work a little harder. Both are available for duplication. The word lists can also be your "calling key" for the bingo games.

FILL IN THE BLANK AND MATCHING
There are 4 each of the fill in the blank and matching worksheets for both the unit and vocabulary words. These pages can be used either as extra worksheets for students or as objective parts of a unit test. They can be done individually if students need extra help or as a whole class activity to review the material covered.

MAGIC SQUARES
The magic squares not only reinforce the material covered but also work on reasoning and math skills. Many teachers have told us that their students really enjoy doing these!

WORD SEARCH PUZZLES
The word search words go in all directions, as indicated on your answer keys. Two of the word search puzzles have the clues listed rather than the words. This makes the puzzle a little more difficult, but it reinforces the material better. Two word search puzzles have words only for students who find the clue puzzles too difficult.

CROSSWORD PUZZLES
Both unit and vocabulary word sections have 4 crossword puzzles.

BINGO CARDS
There are 32 individual bingo cards for the unit words and 32 individual bingo cards for the vocabulary words. You can use your word list as a "call list," calling the words at random and marking them off of your list as you go, or you could use the flash cards by cutting them apart and drawing the words at random from a hat (or box or whatever). To make a better review, you might ask for the definition and spelling of each word as you call it out–or you could call out the definitions and have students tell you the words they need to look for on the puzzle.

JUGGLE LETTERS
The vocabulary juggle letter game is intended to help students learn the spellings of the words. One sheet has the definitions listed on it as an extra help for students who need it or to reinforce the definitions if you choose to do so.

FLASH CARDS
We've included a set of vocabulary flash cards you can duplicate, cut, and fold for your students. Some teachers make a few sets for general use by the class; others make a set for each student. Some teachers duplicate them for each student and have the students cut & fold their own. You can cut out just the words and put them in a hat, have each student pick out one word and write the definition and a sentence for that word. Students then swap words and papers, with the next student adding a sentence of his own under the last one. You can have students swap as many times as you like. Each time the student will read the sentences written prior to his own and then add a sentence. You can cut out the words and definitions separately and play "I Have; Who Has?" Each student in the room draws a word and definition. The first student says, "I have (the name of the word). Who has the definition?" The student with the definition reads it then says, "I have (the name of the vocabulary word she has). Who has the definition?" The round continues until all words and definitions have been given.

Macbeth Unit Word List

No.	Word	Clue/Definition
1.	BANQUO	Macbeth had him killed because he suspected Macbeth killed Duncan
2.	BELL	Lady Macbeth's signal to Macbeth
3.	BODY	Macduff discovered Duncan's dead one
4.	BRANCHES	Malcolm's army uses them as camouflage
5.	CHILD	The witches showed Macbeth a bloody _____.
6.	COUSIN	Macbeth to Duncan
7.	DAGGERS	There's _____ in men's smiles.
8.	DAY	The night is long that never finds the _____.
9.	DESIRES	Stars, hide your fires,/Let not light see my black and deep _____.
10.	DONALBAIN	In line for the throne after Malcolm
11.	DUNCAN	King of Scotland; murdered by Macbeth
12.	ENGLAND	Malcolm fled to this country
13.	FLEANCE	He escapes Macbeth's murder plot, but Banquo does not
14.	FOUL	Fair is _____, and _____ is fair.
15.	GHOST	Macbeth saw Banquo's at the banquet table
16.	GLAMIS	Macbeth's original title, Thane of _____.
17.	HEAD	The witches showed Macbeth an armed _____.
18.	HECATE	Queen of witches
19.	IRELAND	Donalbain flees there
20.	KINGS	The witches showed Macbeth eight _____.
21.	LADY MACBETH	Encourages Macbeth to kill Duncan
22.	LEAVING	Nothing in his life/Became him like the _____ it.
23.	LENNOX	One of Duncan's noblemen
24.	MACBETH	Kills Duncan to gain the throne
25.	MACDONWALD	Macbeth defeats him, which pleases Duncan
26.	MACDUFF	Kills Macbeth for revenge and to restore the throne to the proper ruler
27.	MALCOLM	Duncan's eldest son
28.	NOTHING	It is a table/Told by an idiot, full of sound and fury,/Signifying _____.
29.	ROBES	Why do you dress me in borrowed _____?
30.	ROSS	Messenger; he told Macduff his family was murdered
31.	SCOTLAND	Country of which Duncan is king
32.	SERPENT	Look like the innocent flower/But be the _____ under't.
33.	SHAKESPEARE	Author
34.	SIWARD	Attemtps to kill Macbeth, but he is slain
35.	SLEEP	One thing drinking provokes
36.	STARS	But signs of nobleness, like _____, shall shine/On all deservers.
37.	THANE	_____ of Cawdor
38.	THUMB	By the pricking of my _____,/Something wicked this way comes.
39.	TIME	The _____ is free.
40.	TROUBLE	Double, double toil and _____
41.	VISIONS	Hecate wants the witches to give Macbeth these false impressions
42.	WITCHES	Hecate is their queen

Macbeth Fill In The Blank 1

_____

_____

_____

_____

_____

_____

_____

_____

_____

_____

_____

_____

_____

_____

_____

_____

_____

_____

_____

_____

1. Double, double toil and _____
2. In line for the throne after Malcolm
3. Macbeth's original title, Thane of _____.
4. Lady Macbeth's signal to Macbeth
5. Kills Duncan to gain the throne
6. Queen of witches
7. But signs of nobleness, like _____, shall shine/On all deservers.
8. Malcolm's army uses them as camouflage
9. Hecate wants the witches to give Macbeth these false impressions
10. Encourages Macbeth to kill Duncan
11. Look like the innocent flower/But be the _____ under't.
12. Macduff discovered Duncan's dead one
13. _____ of Cawdor
14. There's _____ in men's smiles.
15. It is a table/Told by an idiot, full of sound and fury,/Signifying _____.
16. The night is long that never finds the _____.
17. The _____ is free.
18. By the pricking of my _____,/Something wicked this way comes.
19. Kills Macbeth for revenge and to restore the throne to the proper ruler
20. The witches showed Macbeth eight _____.

Macbeth Fill In The Blank 1 Answer Key

TROUBLE	1. Double, double toil and _____
DONALBAIN	2. In line for the throne after Malcolm
GLAMIS	3. Macbeth's original title, Thane of _____.
BELL	4. Lady Macbeth's signal to Macbeth
MACBETH	5. Kills Duncan to gain the throne
HECATE	6. Queen of witches
STARS	7. But signs of nobleness, like _____, shall shine/On all deservers.
BRANCHES	8. Malcolm's army uses them as camouflage
VISIONS	9. Hecate wants the witches to give Macbeth these false impressions
LADY MACBETH	10. Encourages Macbeth to kill Duncan
SERPENT	11. Look like the innocent flower/But be the _____ under't.
BODY	12. Macduff discovered Duncan's dead one
THANE	13. _____ of Cawdor
DAGGERS	14. There's _____ in men's smiles.
NOTHING	15. It is a tale/Told by an idiot, full of sound and fury,/Signifying _____.
DAY	16. The night is long that never finds the _____.
TIME	17. The _____ is free.
THUMB	18. By the pricking of my _____,/Something wicked this way comes.
MACDUFF	19. Kills Macbeth for revenge and to restore the throne to the proper ruler
KINGS	20. The witches showed Macbeth eight _____.

Macbeth Fill In The Blank 2

_____

1. One thing drinking provokes
2. Macbeth saw Banquo's ____ at the banquet table
3. Malcolm's army uses them as camouflage
4. But signs of nobleness, like _____, shall shine/On all deservers.
5. Macduff discovered Duncan's dead one
6. Macbeth's original title, Thane of _____.
7. Duncan's eldest son
8. Kills Duncan to gain the throne
9. The _____ is free.
10. The night is long that never finds the _____.
11. Lady Macbeth's signal to Macbeth
12. Double, double toil and _____
13. Fair is _____, and _____ is fair.
14. Encourages Macbeth to kill Duncan
15. He escapes Macbeth's murder plot, but Banquo does not
16. Country of which Duncan is king
17. Hecate is their queen
18. The witches showed Macbeth an armed _____.
19. Messenger; he told Macduff his family was murdered
20. Donalbain flees there

Macbeth Fill In The Blank 2 Answer Key

SLEEP	1. One thing drinking provokes
GHOST	2. Macbeth saw Banquo's at the banquet table
BRANCHES	3. Malcolm's army uses them as camouflage
STARS	4. But signs of nobleness, like _____, shall shine/On all deservers.
BODY	5. Macduff discovered Duncan's dead one
GLAMIS	6. Macbeth's original title, Thane of _____.
MALCOLM	7. Duncan's eldest son
MACBETH	8. Kills Duncan to gain the throne
TIME	9. The _____ is free.
DAY	10. The night is long that never finds the _____.
BELL	11. Lady Macbeth's signal to Macbeth
TROUBLE	12. Double, double toil and _____
FOUL	13. Fair is _____, and _____ is fair.
LADY MACBETH	14. Encourages Macbeth to kill Duncan
FLEANCE	15. He escapes Macbeth's murder plot, but Banquo does not
SCOTLAND	16. Country of which Duncan is king
WITCHES	17. Hecate is their queen
HEAD	18. The witches showed Macbeth an armed _____.
ROSS	19. Messenger; he told Macduff his family was murdered
IRELAND	20. Donalbain flees there

Macbeth Fill In The Blank 3

_____

_____

_____

_____

_____

_____

_____

_____

_____

_____

_____

_____

_____

_____

_____

_____

_____

_____

_____

_____

1. Author
2. Fair is _____, and _____ is fair.
3. Double, double toil and _____
4. The witches showed Macbeth eight _____.
5. Stars, hide your fires,/Let not light see my black and deep _____.
6. Macbeth to Duncan
7. Kills Macbeth for revenge and to restore the throne to the proper ruler
8. Donalbain flees there
9. Malcolm's army uses them as camouflage
10. Macbeth had him killed because he suspected Macbeth killed Duncan
11. One thing drinking provokes
12. Hecate is their queen
13. Encourages Macbeth to kill Duncan
14. Malcolm fled to this country
15. Macduff discovered Duncan's dead one
16. It is a tale/Told by an idiot, full of sound and fury,/Signifying _____.
17. The witches showed Macbeth an armed _____.
18. Kills Duncan to gain the throne
19. King of Scotland; murdered by Macbeth
20. The witches showed Macbeth a bloody _____.

Macbeth Fill In The Blank 3 Answer Key

SHAKESPEARE	1. Author
FOUL	2. Fair is _____, and _____ is fair.
TROUBLE	3. Double, double toil and _____
KINGS	4. The witches showed Macbeth eight _____.
DESIRES	5. Stars, hide your fires,/Let not light see my black and deep _____.
COUSIN	6. Macbeth to Duncan
MACDUFF	7. Kills Macbeth for revenge and to restore the throne to the proper ruler
IRELAND	8. Donalbain flees there
BRANCHES	9. Malcolm's army uses them as camouflage
BANQUO	10. Macbeth had him killed because he suspected Macbeth killed Duncan
SLEEP	11. One thing drinking provokes
WITCHES	12. Hecate is their queen
LADY MACBETH	13. Encourages Macbeth to kill Duncan
ENGLAND	14. Malcolm fled to this country
BODY	15. Macduff discovered Duncan's dead one
NOTHING	16. It is a tale/Told by an idiot, full of sound and fury,/Signifying _____.
HEAD	17. The witches showed Macbeth an armed _____.
MACBETH	18. Kills Duncan to gain the throne
DUNCAN	19. King of Scotland; murdered by Macbeth
CHILD	20. The witches showed Macbeth a bloody _____.

Macbeth Fill In The Blank 4

_____

_____

_____

_____

_____

_____

_____

_____

_____

_____

_____

_____

_____

_____

_____

_____

_____

_____

_____

_____

1. Messenger; he told Macduff his family was murdered
2. It is a tale/Told by an idiot, full of sound and fury,/Signifying _____.
3. One of Duncan's noblemen
4. Macbeth to Duncan
5. There's _____ in men's smiles.
6. Duncan's eldest son
7. The night is long that never finds the _____.
8. Author
9. Kills Duncan to gain the throne
10. Attemtps to kill Macbeth, but he is slain
11. But signs of nobleness, like _____, shall shine/On all deservers.
12. The witches showed Macbeth eight _____.
13. Malcolm's army uses them as camouflage
14. Macbeth defeats him, which pleases Duncan
15. The _____ is free.
16. Kills Macbeth for revenge and to restore the throne to the proper ruler
17. The witches showed Macbeth a bloody _____.
18. Macduff discovered Duncan's dead one
19. Double, double toil and _____
20. Why do you dress me in borrowed _____?

Macbeth Fill In The Blank 4 Answer Key

ROSS	1. Messenger; he told Macduff his family was murdered
NOTHING	2. It is a tale/Told by an idiot, full of sound and fury,/Signifying _____.
LENNOX	3. One of Duncan's noblemen
COUSIN	4. Macbeth to Duncan
DAGGERS	5. There's _____ in men's smiles.
MALCOLM	6. Duncan's eldest son
DAY	7. The night is long that never finds the _____.
SHAKESPEARE	8. Author
MACBETH	9. Kills Duncan to gain the throne
SIWARD	10. Attemtps to kill Macbeth, but he is slain
STARS	11. But signs of nobleness, like _____, shall shine/On all deservers.
KINGS	12. The witches showed Macbeth eight _____.
BRANCHES	13. Malcolm's army uses them as camouflage
MACDONWALD	14. Macbeth defeats him, which pleases Duncan
TIME	15. The _____ is free.
MACDUFF	16. Kills Macbeth for revenge and to restore the throne to the proper ruler
CHILD	17. The witches showed Macbeth a bloody _____.
BODY	18. Macduff discovered Duncan's dead one
TROUBLE	19. Double, double toil and _____
ROBES	20. Why do you dress me in borrowed _____?

Macbeth Matching 1

___ 1. SHAKESPEARE
___ 2. MACDONWALD
___ 3. ROBES
___ 4. THANE
___ 5. LADY MACBETH
___ 6. STARS
___ 7. FOUL
___ 8. BODY
___ 9. BANQUO
___ 10. WITCHES
___ 11. TIME
___ 12. SIWARD
___ 13. BRANCHES
___ 14. MACDUFF
___ 15. SCOTLAND
___ 16. HEAD
___ 17. LENNOX
___ 18. BELL
___ 19. SERPENT
___ 20. MACBETH
___ 21. DAY
___ 22. CHILD
___ 23. ROSS
___ 24. LEAVING
___ 25. THUMB

A. Kills Macbeth for revenge and to restore the throne to the proper ruler
B. Encourages Macbeth to kill Duncan
C. Malcolm's army uses them as camouflage
D. Kills Duncan to gain the throne
E. Country of which Duncan is king
F. The night is long that never finds the _____.
G. _____ of Cawdor
H. By the pricking of my _____,/Something wicked this way comes.
I. Look like the innocent flower/But be the _____ under't.
J. Why do you dress me in borrowed _____?
K. Fair is _____, and _____ is fair.
L. One of Duncan's noblemen
M. Attemtps to kill Macbeth, but he is slain
N. Nothing in his life/Became him like the _____ it.
O. The witches showed Macbeth a bloody _____.
P. The witches showed Macbeth an armed _____.
Q. Hecate is their queen
R. The _____ is free.
S. Macbeth defeats him, which pleases Duncan
T. Lady Macbeth's signal to Macbeth
U. Author
V. Messenger; he told Macduff his family was murdered
W. Macduff discovered Duncan's dead one
X. Macbeth had him killed because he suspected Macbeth killed Duncan
Y. But signs of nobleness, like _____, shall shine/On all deservers.

Macbeth Matching 1 Answer Key

U - 1. SHAKESPEARE	A.	Kills Macbeth for revenge and to restore the throne to the proper ruler
S - 2. MACDONWALD	B.	Encourages Macbeth to kill Duncan
J - 3. ROBES	C.	Malcolm's army uses them as camouflage
G - 4. THANE	D.	Kills Duncan to gain the throne
B - 5. LADY MACBETH	E.	Country of which Duncan is king
Y - 6. STARS	F.	The night is long that never finds the _____.
K - 7. FOUL	G.	_____ of Cawdor
W - 8. BODY	H.	By the pricking of my _____./Something wicked this way comes.
X - 9. BANQUO	I.	Look like the innocent flower/But be the _____ under't.
Q -10. WITCHES	J.	Why do you dress me in borrowed _____?
R -11. TIME	K.	Fair is _____, and _____ is fair.
M -12. SIWARD	L.	One of Duncan's noblemen
C -13. BRANCHES	M.	Attemtps to kill Macbeth, but he is slain
A -14. MACDUFF	N.	Nothing in his life/Became him like the _____ it.
E -15. SCOTLAND	O.	The witches showed Macbeth a bloody _____.
P -16. HEAD	P.	The witches showed Macbeth an armed _____.
L -17. LENNOX	Q.	Hecate is their queen
T -18. BELL	R.	The _____ is free.
I -19. SERPENT	S.	Macbeth defeats him, which pleases Duncan
D -20. MACBETH	T.	Lady Macbeth's signal to Macbeth
F -21. DAY	U.	Author
O -22. CHILD	V.	Messenger; he told Macduff his family was murdered
V -23. ROSS	W.	Macduff discovered Duncan's dead one
N -24. LEAVING	X.	Macbeth had him killed because he suspected Macbeth killed Duncan
H -25. THUMB	Y.	But signs of nobleness, like _____, shall shine/On all deservers.

Copyrighted

Macbeth Matching 2

___ 1. SHAKESPEARE
___ 2. VISIONS
___ 3. SIWARD
___ 4. ROBES
___ 5. HEAD
___ 6. SLEEP
___ 7. BANQUO
___ 8. LENNOX
___ 9. KINGS
___10. MACBETH
___11. ROSS
___12. BRANCHES
___13. MACDONWALD
___14. BODY
___15. DUNCAN
___16. TROUBLE
___17. FLEANCE
___18. GHOST
___19. THANE
___20. DAGGERS
___21. MACDUFF
___22. HECATE
___23. NOTHING
___24. LADY MACBETH
___25. GLAMIS

A. There's _____ in men's smiles.
B. Attemtps to kill Macbeth, but he is slain
C. Macbeth saw Banquo's at the banquet table
D. Macbeth defeats him, which pleases Duncan
E. King of Scotland; murdered by Macbeth
F. Macbeth's original title, Thane of _____.
G. Kills Macbeth for revenge and to restore the throne to the proper ruler
H. One of Duncan's noblemen
I. Macduff discovered Duncan's dead one
J. He escapes Macbeth's murder plot, but Banquo does not
K. Malcolm's army uses them as camouflage
L. Author
M. Encourages Macbeth to kill Duncan
N. One thing drinking provokes
O. Why do you dress me in borrowed _____?
P. Kills Duncan to gain the throne
Q. Double, double toil and _____
R. _____ of Cawdor
S. Queen of witches
T. The witches showed Macbeth an armed _____.
U. Hecate wants the witches to give Macbeth these false impressions
V. Messenger; he told Macduff his family was murdered
W. The witches showed Macbeth eight _____.
X. Macbeth had him killed because he suspected Macbeth killed Duncan
Y. It is a tale/Told by an idiot, full of sound and fury,/Signifying _____.

Macbeth Matching 2 Answer Key

L - 1. SHAKESPEARE
U - 2. VISIONS
B - 3. SIWARD
O - 4. ROBES
T - 5. HEAD
N - 6. SLEEP
X - 7. BANQUO
H - 8. LENNOX
W - 9. KINGS
P - 10. MACBETH
V - 11. ROSS
K - 12. BRANCHES
D - 13. MACDONWALD
I - 14. BODY
E - 15. DUNCAN
Q - 16. TROUBLE
J - 17. FLEANCE
C - 18. GHOST
R - 19. THANE
A - 20. DAGGERS
G - 21. MACDUFF
S - 22. HECATE
Y - 23. NOTHING
M - 24. LADY MACBETH
F - 25. GLAMIS

A. There's _____ in men's smiles.
B. Attemtps to kill Macbeth, but he is slain
C. Macbeth saw Banquo's at the banquet table
D. Macbeth defeats him, which pleases Duncan
E. King of Scotland; murdered by Macbeth
F. Macbeth's original title, Thane of _____.
G. Kills Macbeth for revenge and to restore the throne to the proper ruler
H. One of Duncan's noblemen
I. Macduff discovered Duncan's dead one
J. He escapes Macbeth's murder plot, but Banquo does not
K. Malcolm's army uses them as camouflage
L. Author
M. Encourages Macbeth to kill Duncan
N. One thing drinking provokes
O. Why do you dress me in borrowed _____?
P. Kills Duncan to gain the throne
Q. Double, double toil and _____
R. _____ of Cawdor
S. Queen of witches
T. The witches showed Macbeth an armed _____.
U. Hecate wants the witches to give Macbeth these false impressions
V. Messenger; he told Macduff his family was murdered
W. The witches showed Macbeth eight _____.
X. Macbeth had him killed because he suspected Macbeth killed Duncan
Y. It is a tale/Told by an idiot, full of sound and fury,/Signifying _____.

Macbeth Matching 3

___ 1. DESIRES
___ 2. GHOST
___ 3. HECATE
___ 4. BRANCHES
___ 5. SIWARD
___ 6. HEAD
___ 7. TIME
___ 8. VISIONS
___ 9. KINGS
___ 10. BANQUO
___ 11. MALCOLM
___ 12. MACDONWALD
___ 13. DAY
___ 14. DAGGERS
___ 15. ROSS
___ 16. DUNCAN
___ 17. THUMB
___ 18. ROBES
___ 19. STARS
___ 20. COUSIN
___ 21. FLEANCE
___ 22. IRELAND
___ 23. TROUBLE
___ 24. LADY MACBETH
___ 25. THANE

A. There's _____ in men's smiles.
B. Macbeth defeats him, which pleases Duncan
C. Macbeth had him killed because he suspected Macbeth killed Duncan
D. Encourages Macbeth to kill Duncan
E. By the pricking of my _____,/Something wicked this way comes.
F. But signs of nobleness, like _____, shall shine/On all deservers.
G. _____ of Cawdor
H. Donalbain flees there
I. He escapes Macbeth's murder plot, but Banquo does not
J. Attemtps to kill Macbeth, but he is slain
K. Malcolm's army uses them as camouflage
L. Stars, hide your fires,/Let not light see my black and deep _____.
M. Duncan's eldest son
N. Hecate wants the witches to give Macbeth these false impressions
O. Macbeth saw Banquo's at the banquet table
P. Double, double toil and _____
Q. The _____ is free.
R. Messenger; he told Macduff his family was murdered
S. Macbeth to Duncan
T. The night is long that never finds the _____.
U. The witches showed Macbeth an armed _____.
V. King of Scotland; murdered by Macbeth
W. Why do you dress me in borrowed _____?
X. Queen of witches
Y. The witches showed Macbeth eight _____.

Macbeth Matching 3 Answer Key

L - 1. DESIRES	A. There's _____ in men's smiles.
O - 2. GHOST	B. Macbeth defeats him, which pleases Duncan
X - 3. HECATE	C. Macbeth had him killed because he suspected Macbeth killed Duncan
K - 4. BRANCHES	D. Encourages Macbeth to kill Duncan
J - 5. SIWARD	E. By the pricking of my _____,/Something wicked this way comes.
U - 6. HEAD	F. But signs of nobleness, like _____, shall shine/On all deservers.
Q - 7. TIME	G. _____ of Cawdor
N - 8. VISIONS	H. Donalbain flees there
Y - 9. KINGS	I. He escapes Macbeth's murder plot, but Banquo does not
C - 10. BANQUO	J. Attemtps to kill Macbeth, but he is slain
M - 11. MALCOLM	K. Malcolm's army uses them as camouflage
B - 12. MACDONWALD	L. Stars, hide your fires,/Let not light see my black and deep _____.
T - 13. DAY	M. Duncan's eldest son
A - 14. DAGGERS	N. Hecate wants the witches to give Macbeth these false impressions
R - 15. ROSS	O. Macbeth saw Banquo's at the banquet table
V - 16. DUNCAN	P. Double, double toil and _____
E - 17. THUMB	Q. The _____ is free.
W - 18. ROBES	R. Messenger; he told Macduff his family was murdered
F - 19. STARS	S. Macbeth to Duncan
S - 20. COUSIN	T. The night is long that never finds the _____.
I - 21. FLEANCE	U. The witches showed Macbeth an armed _____.
H - 22. IRELAND	V. King of Scotland; murdered by Macbeth
P - 23. TROUBLE	W. Why do you dress me in borrowed _____?
D - 24. LADY MACBETH	X. Queen of witches
G - 25. THANE	Y. The witches showed Macbeth eight _____.

Macbeth Matching 4

___ 1. MALCOLM   A. Macbeth to Duncan
___ 2. BRANCHES   B. One thing drinking provokes
___ 3. KINGS   C. The _____ is free.
___ 4. MACDUFF   D. The witches showed Macbeth eight _____.
___ 5. MACDONWALD   E. The witches showed Macbeth a bloody _____.
___ 6. STARS   F. Duncan's eldest son
___ 7. MACBETH   G. Macbeth's original title, Thane of _____.
___ 8. TIME   H. Malcolm's army uses them as camouflage
___ 9. BANQUO   I. King of Scotland; murdered by Macbeth
___ 10. GLAMIS   J. Kills Macbeth for revenge and to restore the throne to the proper ruler
___ 11. LENNOX   K. By the pricking of my _____,/Something wicked this way comes.
___ 12. SIWARD   L. Lady Macbeth's signal to Macbeth
___ 13. DUNCAN   M. The witches showed Macbeth an armed _____.
___ 14. FLEANCE   N. Attemtps to kill Macbeth, but he is slain
___ 15. THANE   O. Kills Duncan to gain the throne
___ 16. LEAVING   P. _____ of Cawdor
___ 17. BELL   Q. He escapes Macbeth's murder plot, but Banquo does not
___ 18. HEAD   R. Macbeth had him killed because he suspected Macbeth killed Duncan
___ 19. COUSIN   S. Messenger; he told Macduff his family was murdered
___ 20. THUMB   T. One of Duncan's noblemen
___ 21. IRELAND   U. Nothing in his life/Became him like the _____ it.
___ 22. DAY   V. The night is long that never finds the _____.
___ 23. ROSS   W. But signs of nobleness, like _____, shall shine/On all deservers.
___ 24. CHILD   X. Macbeth defeats him, which pleases Duncan
___ 25. SLEEP   Y. Donalbain flees there

Macbeth Matching 4 Answer Key

F - 1. MALCOLM		A. Macbeth to Duncan
H - 2. BRANCHES		B. One thing drinking provokes
D - 3. KINGS		C. The _____ is free.
J - 4. MACDUFF		D. The witches showed Macbeth eight _____.
X - 5. MACDONWALD		E. The witches showed Macbeth a bloody _____.
W - 6. STARS		F. Duncan's eldest son
O - 7. MACBETH		G. Macbeth's original title, Thane of _____.
C - 8. TIME		H. Malcolm's army uses them as camouflage
R - 9. BANQUO		I. King of Scotland; murdered by Macbeth
G - 10. GLAMIS		J. Kills Macbeth for revenge and to restore the throne to the proper ruler
T - 11. LENNOX		K. By the pricking of my _____,/Something wicked this way comes.
N - 12. SIWARD		L. Lady Macbeth's signal to Macbeth
I - 13. DUNCAN		M. The witches showed Macbeth an armed _____.
Q - 14. FLEANCE		N. Attemtps to kill Macbeth, but he is slain
P - 15. THANE		O. Kills Duncan to gain the throne
U - 16. LEAVING		P. _____ of Cawdor
L - 17. BELL		Q. He escapes Macbeth's murder plot, but Banquo does not
M - 18. HEAD		R. Macbeth had him killed because he suspected Macbeth killed Duncan
A - 19. COUSIN		S. Messenger; he told Macduff his family was murdered
K - 20. THUMB		T. One of Duncan's noblemen
Y - 21. IRELAND		U. Nothing in his life/Became him like the _____ it.
V - 22. DAY		V. The night is long that never finds the _____.
S - 23. ROSS		W. But signs of nobleness, like _____, shall shine/On all deservers.
E - 24. CHILD		X. Macbeth defeats him, which pleases Duncan
B - 25. SLEEP		Y. Donalbain flees there

Macbeth Magic Squares 1

Match the definition with the vocabulary word. Put your answers in the magic squares below. When your answers are correct, all columns and rows will add to the same number.

A. SHAKESPEARE E. LEAVING   I. LADY MACBETH M. TROUBLE
B. DESIRES   F. BANQUO   J. MACBETH   N. THANE
C. DAY   G. FLEANCE   K. KINGS   O. SIWARD
D. WITCHES   H. LENNOX   L. BODY   P. CHILD

1. Author
2. _____ of Cawdor
3. Kills Duncan to gain the throne
4. Nothing in his life/Became him like the _____ it.
5. He escapes Macbeth's murder plot, but Banquo does not
6. Macduff discovered Duncan's dead one
7. The witches showed Macbeth a bloody _____.
8. The night is long that never finds the _____.
9. Attemtps to kill Macbeth, but he is slain
10. Hecate is their queen
11. One of Duncan's noblemen
12. The witches showed Macbeth eight _____.
13. Encourages Macbeth to kill Duncan
14. Macbeth had him killed because he suspected Macbeth killed Duncan
15. Stars, hide your fires,/Let not light see my black and deep _____.
16. Double, double toil and _____

A=	B=	C=	D=
E=	F=	G=	H=
I=	J=	K=	L=
M=	N=	O=	P=

Macbeth Magic Squares 1 Answer Key

Match the definition with the vocabulary word. Put your answers in the magic squares below. When your answers are correct, all columns and rows will add to the same number.

A. SHAKESPEARE E. LEAVING   I. LADY MACBETH   M. TROUBLE
B. DESIRES   F. BANQUO   J. MACBETH   N. THANE
C. DAY   G. FLEANCE   K. KINGS   O. SIWARD
D. WITCHES   H. LENNOX   L. BODY   P. CHILD

1. Author
2. _____ of Cawdor
3. Kills Duncan to gain the throne
4. Nothing in his life/Became him like the _____ it.
5. He escapes Macbeth's murder plot, but Banquo does not
6. Macduff discovered Duncan's dead one
7. The witches showed Macbeth a bloody _____.
8. The night is long that never finds the _____.
9. Attemtps to kill Macbeth, but he is slain
10. Hecate is their queen
11. One of Duncan's noblemen
12. The witches showed Macbeth eight _____.
13. Encourages Macbeth to kill Duncan
14. Macbeth had him killed because he suspected Macbeth killed Duncan
15. Stars, hide your fires,/Let not light see my black and deep _____.
16. Double, double toil and _____

A=1	B=15	C=8	D=10
E=4	F=14	G=5	H=11
I=13	J=3	K=12	L=6
M=16	N=2	O=9	P=7

Macbeth Magic Squares 2

Match the definition with the vocabulary word. Put your answers in the magic squares below. When your answers are correct, all columns and rows will add to the same number.

A. IRELAND   E. HECATE   I. MACBETH   M. VISIONS
B. LADY MACBETH   F. MACDUFF   J. FOUL   N. TIME
C. SERPENT   G. MALCOLM   K. DUNCAN   O. COUSIN
D. GHOST   H. LENNOX   L. GLAMIS   P. NOTHING

1. Kills Macbeth for revenge and to restore the throne to the proper ruler
2. Kills Duncan to gain the throne
3. Macbeth to Duncan
4. Macbeth saw Banquo's at the banquet table
5. Hecate wants the witches to give Macbeth these false impressions
6. Encourages Macbeth to kill Duncan
7. One of Duncan's noblemen
8. King of Scotland; murdered by Macbeth
9. Look like the innocent flower/But be the _____ under't.
10. It is a tale/Told by an idiot, full of sound and fury,/Signifying _____.
11. Fair is _____, and _____ is fair.
12. Queen of witches
13. Macbeth's original title, Thane of _____.
14. Duncan's eldest son
15. Donalbain flees there
16. The _____ is free.

A=	B=	C=	D=
E=	F=	G=	H=
I=	J=	K=	L=
M=	N=	O=	P=

Macbeth Magic Squares 2 Answer Key

Match the definition with the vocabulary word. Put your answers in the magic squares below. When your answers are correct, all columns and rows will add to the same number.

A. IRELAND
B. LADY MACBETH
C. SERPENT
D. GHOST
E. HECATE
F. MACDUFF
G. MALCOLM
H. LENNOX
I. MACBETH
J. FOUL
K. DUNCAN
L. GLAMIS
M. VISIONS
N. TIME
O. COUSIN
P. NOTHING

1. Kills Macbeth for revenge and to restore the throne to the proper ruler
2. Kills Duncan to gain the throne
3. Macbeth to Duncan
4. Macbeth saw Banquo's at the banquet table
5. Hecate wants the witches to give Macbeth these false impressions
6. Encourages Macbeth to kill Duncan
7. One of Duncan's noblemen
8. King of Scotland; murdered by Macbeth
9. Look like the innocent flower/But be the _____ under't.
10. It is a tale/Told by an idiot, full of sound and fury,/Signifying _____.
11. Fair is _____, and _____ is fair.
12. Queen of witches
13. Macbeth's original title, Thane of _____.
14. Duncan's eldest son
15. Donalbain flees there
16. The _____ is free.

A=15	B=6	C=9	D=4
E=12	F=1	G=14	H=7
I=2	J=11	K=8	L=13
M=5	N=16	O=3	P=10

Macbeth Magic Squares 3

Match the definition with the vocabulary word. Put your answers in the magic squares below. When your answers are correct, all columns and rows will add to the same number.

A. SHAKESPEARE
B. VISIONS
C. MACDONWALD
D. LEAVING
E. MACBETH
F. FLEANCE
G. COUSIN
H. SLEEP
I. DONALBAIN
J. DAGGERS
K. SERPENT
L. BODY
M. IRELAND
N. ROSS
O. ROBES
P. MACDUFF

1. One thing drinking provokes
2. Author
3. Hecate wants the witches to give Macbeth these false impressions
4. Macbeth to Duncan
5. There's _____ in men's smiles.
6. Why do you dress me in borrowed _____?
7. Kills Macbeth for revenge and to restore the throne to the proper ruler
8. In line for the throne after Malcolm
9. Look like the innocent flower/But be the _____ under't.
10. Messenger; he told Macduff his family was murdered
11. Donalbain flees there
12. Macduff discovered Duncan's dead one
13. Kills Duncan to gain the throne
14. Nothing in his life/Became him like the _____ it.
15. Macbeth defeats him, which pleases Duncan
16. He escapes Macbeth's murder plot, but Banquo does not

A=	B=	C=	D=
E=	F=	G=	H=
I=	J=	K=	L=
M=	N=	O=	P=

Macbeth Magic Squares 3 Answer Key

Match the definition with the vocabulary word. Put your answers in the magic squares below. When your answers are correct, all columns and rows will add to the same number.

A. SHAKESPEARE
B. VISIONS
C. MACDONWALD
D. LEAVING
E. MACBETH
F. FLEANCE
G. COUSIN
H. SLEEP
I. DONALBAIN
J. DAGGERS
K. SERPENT
L. BODY
M. IRELAND
N. ROSS
O. ROBES
P. MACDUFF

1. One thing drinking provokes
2. Author
3. Hecate wants the witches to give Macbeth these false impressions
4. Macbeth to Duncan
5. There's _____ in men's smiles.
6. Why do you dress me in borrowed _____?
7. Kills Macbeth for revenge and to restore the throne to the proper ruler
8. In line for the throne after Malcolm
9. Look like the innocent flower/But be the _____ under't.
10. Messenger; he told Macduff his family was murdered
11. Donalbain flees there
12. Macduff discovered Duncan's dead one
13. Kills Duncan to gain the throne
14. Nothing in his life/Became him like the _____ it.
15. Macbeth defeats him, which pleases Duncan
16. He escapes Macbeth's murder plot, but Banquo does not

A=2	B=3	C=15	D=14
E=13	F=16	G=4	H=1
I=8	J=5	K=9	L=12
M=11	N=10	O=6	P=7

Macbeth Magic Squares 4

Match the definition with the vocabulary word. Put your answers in the magic squares below. When your answers are correct, all columns and rows will add to the same number.

A. BELL
B. MACBETH
C. GLAMIS
D. NOTHING
E. THUMB
F. FOUL
G. ROBES
H. ROSS
I. ENGLAND
J. LADY MACBETH
K. SLEEP
L. MALCOLM
M. DONALBAIN
N. STARS
O. SERPENT
P. MACDUFF

1. In line for the throne after Malcolm
2. Fair is _____, and _____ is fair.
3. Messenger; he told Macduff his family was murdered
4. Look like the innocent flower/But be the _____ under't.
5. Duncan's eldest son
6. Macbeth's original title, Thane of _____.
7. Lady Macbeth's signal to Macbeth
8. Encourages Macbeth to kill Duncan
9. One thing drinking provokes
10. It is a tale/Told by an idiot, full of sound and fury,/Signifying _____.
11. Kills Duncan to gain the throne
12. Malcolm fled to this country
13. But signs of nobleness, like _____, shall shine/On all deservers.
14. By the pricking of my _____, Something wicked this way comes.
15. Why do you dress me in borrowed _____?
16. Kills Macbeth for revenge and to restore the throne to the proper ruler

A=	B=	C=	D=
E=	F=	G=	H=
I=	J=	K=	L=
M=	N=	O=	P=

Macbeth Magic Squares 4 Answer Key

Match the definition with the vocabulary word. Put your answers in the magic squares below. When your answers are correct, all columns and rows will add to the same number.

A. BELL
B. MACBETH
C. GLAMIS
D. NOTHING
E. THUMB
F. FOUL
G. ROBES
H. ROSS
I. ENGLAND
J. LADY MACBETH
K. SLEEP
L. MALCOLM
M. DONALBAIN
N. STARS
O. SERPENT
P. MACDUFF

1. In line for the throne after Malcolm
2. Fair is _____, and _____ is fair.
3. Messenger; he told Macduff his family was murdered
4. Look like the innocent flower/But be the _____ under't.
5. Duncan's eldest son
6. Macbeth's original title, Thane of _____.
7. Lady Macbeth's signal to Macbeth
8. Encourages Macbeth to kill Duncan
9. One thing drinking provokes
10. It is a tale/Told by an idiot, full of sound and fury,/Signifying _____.
11. Kills Duncan to gain the throne
12. Malcolm fled to this country
13. But signs of nobleness, like _____, shall shine/On all deservers.
14. By the pricking of my _____, Something wicked this way comes.
15. Why do you dress me in borrowed _____?
16. Kills Macbeth for revenge and to restore the throne to the proper ruler

A=7	B=11	C=6	D=10
E=14	F=2	G=15	H=3
I=12	J=8	K=9	L=5
M=1	N=13	O=4	P=16

Macbeth Word Search 1

```
T S R W B F R E N G L A N D Q D C S
S R Q H E T O G H O P R F T U A H S
O I O W L B F U B R T P O N M Y I Z
H G W U L R M L L D L H C S V C L M
G L T A B H O A E P E A I I S O D W
W A S H R L T B C A N S S N Z U L T
Z M Q P A D E D E D N I I Y G S A C
F I T Y Y N Q O Y S O C X R H I D G
L S Z Y B J E N H N X N E D E N Y P
Y R C M J Z Q A S K T S W J Y S M W
R W U O I R E L A N D M L A R R A L
J H D D T D B B Z B M Q N E L R C Z
T C W F C L C A S S H A G T E D B F
D L R Q V C A I G T E G L A M P E W
B K G N O U Q N A B A M A C B E T H
M K M T S K I S D D D R B E O O H G
Q L T N B K W I T C H E S H L L D D
M Y B R A N C H E S R X T I M E M Y
```

Attemtps to kill Macbeth, but he is slain (6)
But signs of nobleness, like _____, shall shine/On all deservers. (5)
By the pricking of my _____,/Something wicked this way comes. (5)
Country of which Duncan is king (8)
Donalbain flees there (7)
Duncan's eldest son (7)
Encourages Macbeth to kill Duncan (12)
Fair is _____, and _____ is fair. (4)
He escapes Macbeth's murder plot, but Banquo does not (7)
Macbeth's original title, Thane of _____. (6)
Hecate is their queen (7)
Hecate wants the witches to give Macbeth these false impressions (7)
In line for the throne after Malcolm (9)
It is a tale/Told by an idiot, full of sound and fury,/Signifying _____. (7)
Kills Duncan to gain the throne (7)
King of Scotland; murdered by Macbeth (6)
Lady Macbeth's signal to Macbeth (4)
Macbeth defeats him, which pleases Duncan (10)
Macbeth had him killed because he suspected Macbeth killed Duncan (6)
Macbeth saw Banquo's at the banquet table (5)
Macbeth to Duncan (6)
Macduff discovered Duncan's dead one (4)
Malcolm fled to this country (7)
Malcolm's army uses them as camouflage (8)
Messenger; he told Macduff his family was murdered (4)
One of Duncan's noblemen (6)
One thing drinking provokes (5)
Queen of witches (6)
Stars, hide your fires,/Let not light see my black and deep _____. (7)
The _____ is free. (4)
The night is long that never finds the _____. (3)
The witches showed Macbeth a bloody _____. (5)
The witches showed Macbeth an armed _____. (4)
The witches showed Macbeth eight _____. (5)
There's _____ in men's smiles. (7)
Why do you dress me in borrowed _____? (5)
_____ of Cawdor (5)
Double, double toil and _____ (7)

Macbeth Word Search 1 Answer Key

Attemtps to kill Macbeth, but he is slain (6)
But signs of nobleness, like _____, shall shine/On all deservers. (5)
By the pricking of my _____,/Something wicked this way comes. (5)
Country of which Duncan is king (8)
Donalbain flees there (7)
Duncan's eldest son (7)
Encourages Macbeth to kill Duncan (12)
Fair is _____, and _____ is fair. (4)
He escapes Macbeth's murder plot, but Banquo does not (7)
Macbeth's original title, Thane of _____. (6)
Hecate is their queen (7)
Hecate wants the witches to give Macbeth these false impressions (7)
In line for the throne after Malcolm (9)
It is a tale/Told by an idiot, full of sound and fury,/Signifying _____. (7)
Kills Duncan to gain the throne (7)
King of Scotland; murdered by Macbeth (6)
Lady Macbeth's signal to Macbeth (4)
Macbeth defeats him, which pleases Duncan (10)
Macbeth had him killed because he suspected Macbeth killed Duncan (6)
Macbeth saw Banquo's at the banquet table (5)
Macbeth to Duncan (6)
Macduff discovered Duncan's dead one (4)
Malcolm fled to this country (7)
Malcolm's army uses them as camouflage (8)
Messenger; he told Macduff his family was murdered (4)
One of Duncan's noblemen (6)
One thing drinking provokes (5)
Queen of witches (6)
Stars, hide your fires,/Let not light see my black and deep _____. (7)
The _____ is free. (4)
The night is long that never finds the _____. (3)
The witches showed Macbeth a bloody _____. (5)
The witches showed Macbeth an armed _____. (4)
The witches showed Macbeth eight _____. (5)
There's _____ in men's smiles. (7)
Why do you dress me in borrowed _____? (5)
_____ of Cawdor (5)
Double, double toil and _____ (7)

Macbeth Word Search 2

```
B R A N C H E S S E R P E N T X S W
S Q N Q D M F E T C M J Z S H F L F
X C D F I A H X A R Y A O Q U C E Y
R B O T M C G D R D O H C N M S E M
T U H T T A N G S D G B N D B C P Z
L Y N I L A C T E B U G E L U G C B
S G W L L A S D D R A N T S H F K Y
Y B L G L E N N O X S N C H T T F Q
D F N A R K T D N N R R Q A Z R R X
O E L I M Q A A M W L O U N O G Q
B K S E H I B E L J A A Q S O U N R
S E L D A E S H B S Y L L Y S B I Q
D I L T D N V D A N L M C D R L H E
G Y W L J A C Q I O Z O S O P E T X
Y Z C A T H Y E N I U G G J L A O S
L N S Y R T Q W X S N F J P C M N G
K H X W H D Q H I I R I R E L A N D
C H I L D C F N K V R L H R W N N M
```

Attemtps to kill Macbeth, but he is slain (6)
But signs of nobleness, like _____, shall shine/On all deservers. (5)
By the pricking of my _____,/Something wicked this way comes. (5)
Country of which Duncan is king (8)
Donalbain flees there (7)
Duncan's eldest son (7)
Fair is _____, and _____ is fair. (4)
He escapes Macbeth's murder plot, but Banquo does not (7)
Macbeth's original title, Thane of _____. (6)
Hecate is their queen (7)
Hecate wants the witches to give Macbeth these false impressions (7)
In line for the throne after Malcolm (9)
It is a tale/Told by an idiot, full of sound and fury,/Signifying _____. (7)
Kills Macbeth for revenge and to restore the throne to the proper ruler (7)
King of Scotland; murdered by Macbeth (6)
Lady Macbeth's signal to Macbeth (4)
Look like the innocent flower/But be the _____ under't. (7)
Macbeth defeats him, which pleases Duncan (10)
Macbeth had him killed because he suspected Macbeth killed Duncan (6)
Macbeth saw Banquo's at the banquet table (5)
Macbeth to Duncan (6)
Macduff discovered Duncan's dead one (4)
Malcolm fled to this country (7)
Malcolm's army uses them as camouflage (8)
Messenger; he told Macduff his family was murdered (4)
One of Duncan's noblemen (6)
One thing drinking provokes (5)
Queen of witches (6)
Stars, hide your fires,/Let not light see my black and deep _____. (7)
The _____ is free. (4)
The night is long that never finds the _____. (3)
The witches showed Macbeth a bloody _____. (5)
The witches showed Macbeth an armed _____. (4)
The witches showed Macbeth eight _____. (5)
There's _____ in men's smiles. (7)
Why do you dress me in borrowed _____? (5)
_____ of Cawdor (5)
Double, double toil and _____ (7)

Macbeth Word Search 2 Answer Key

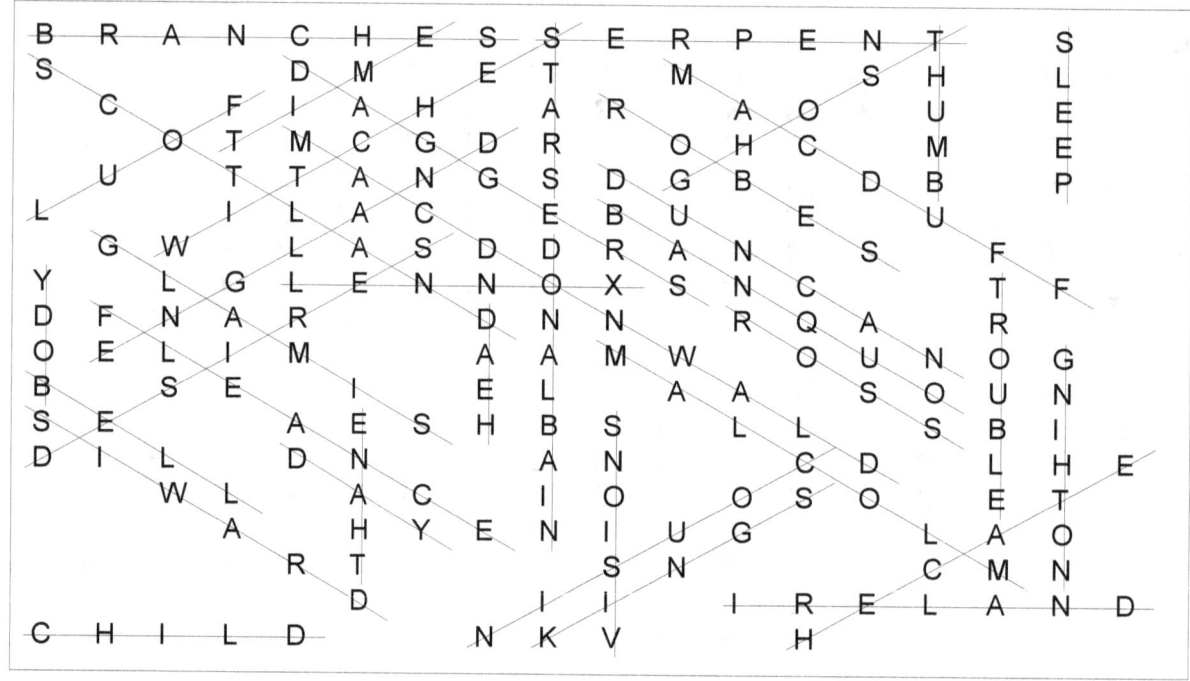

Attemtps to kill Macbeth, but he is slain (6)
But signs of nobleness, like _____, shall shine/On all deservers. (5)
By the pricking of my _____,/Something wicked this way comes. (5)
Country of which Duncan is king (8)
Donalbain flees there (7)
Duncan's eldest son (7)
Fair is _____, and _____ is fair. (4)
He escapes Macbeth's murder plot, but Banquo does not (7)
Macbeth's original title, Thane of _____. (6)
Hecate is their queen (7)
Hecate wants the witches to give Macbeth these false impressions (7)
In line for the throne after Malcolm (9)
It is a tale/Told by an idiot, full of sound and fury,/Signifying _____. (7)
Kills Macbeth for revenge and to restore the throne to the proper ruler (7)
King of Scotland; murdered by Macbeth (6)
Lady Macbeth's signal to Macbeth (4)
Look like the innocent flower/But be the _____ under't. (7)
Macbeth defeats him, which pleases Duncan (10)
Macbeth had him killed because he suspected Macbeth killed Duncan (6)
Macbeth saw Banquo's at the banquet table (5)
Macbeth to Duncan (6)
Macduff discovered Duncan's dead one (4)
Malcolm fled to this country (7)
Malcolm's army uses them as camouflage (8)
Messenger; he told Macduff his family was murdered (4)
One of Duncan's noblemen (6)
One thing drinking provokes (5)
Queen of witches (6)
Stars, hide your fires,/Let not light see my black and deep _____. (7)
The _____ is free. (4)
The night is long that never finds the _____. (3)
The witches showed Macbeth a bloody _____. (5)
The witches showed Macbeth an armed _____. (4)
The witches showed Macbeth eight _____. (5)
There's _____ in men's smiles. (7)
Why do you dress me in borrowed _____? (5)
_____ of Cawdor (5)
Double, double toil and _____ (7)

Macbeth Word Search 3

```
D S W X J W R K H D Q J N X X F R M F X
L E L H V H B S T J L N O M T X M N M L
A Z S M Q Q R M G F V S T N J Y G H L V
W W W I Y P D P B V T Y H S D Z V J V G
N R R F R C F Q P F N L I X K M B C N B
O H R B L E N J T R A P N H M Q P L W B
D H H X V C S Q H D W S G L V D Z N I L
C S P N Q B S G Y V V R L D J R H V T K
A H C Z D G N M F D D Y F Y Y P O N C T
M C Y O C A A C D Z K M Y S D K N B H L
M G N Q T C G Y O S M K F L E A N C E G
P B V X B L X G I U J W T Q X Q H A S G
P M L E E V A W E H S D H F S V V S M S
S U T M T D A N N R A I A G O I Y T A M
C H I L D R B O D Y S L N B N U N A C F
Q T A H D O O V L E L I E G A I L R B J
Y I E K L S Y U R Y K L K N A N L S E S
F R N H E S G P B R L M M B S Q B T G H
H E G E J S E L S L X L A A O L U H N C
M L L A G N P E A O E A F X C D X E O C
R A A D T B T E C M N N G C N D Q C E S
F N N K T A F L A O I H L S U B U G R P
K D D P C S A K D R O S N D D M N F W D
T J F E R M T W V S E H C N A R B X F F
N S H S C S R T T V I S I O N S Q J H Q
```

BANQUO   ENGLAND   LENNOX   SIWARD

BELL   FLEANCE   MACBETH   SLEEP

BODY   FOUL   MACDONWALD   STARS

BRANCHES   GHOST   MACDUFF   THANE

CHILD   GLAMIS   MALCOLM   THUMB

COUSIN   HEAD   NOTHING   TIME

DAGGERS   HECATE   ROBES   TROUBLE

DAY   IRELAND   ROSS   VISIONS

DESIRES   KINGS   SCOTLAND   WITCHES

DONALBAIN   LADY MACBETH   SERPENT

DUNCAN   LEAVING   SHAKESPEARE

Macbeth Word Search 3 Answer Key

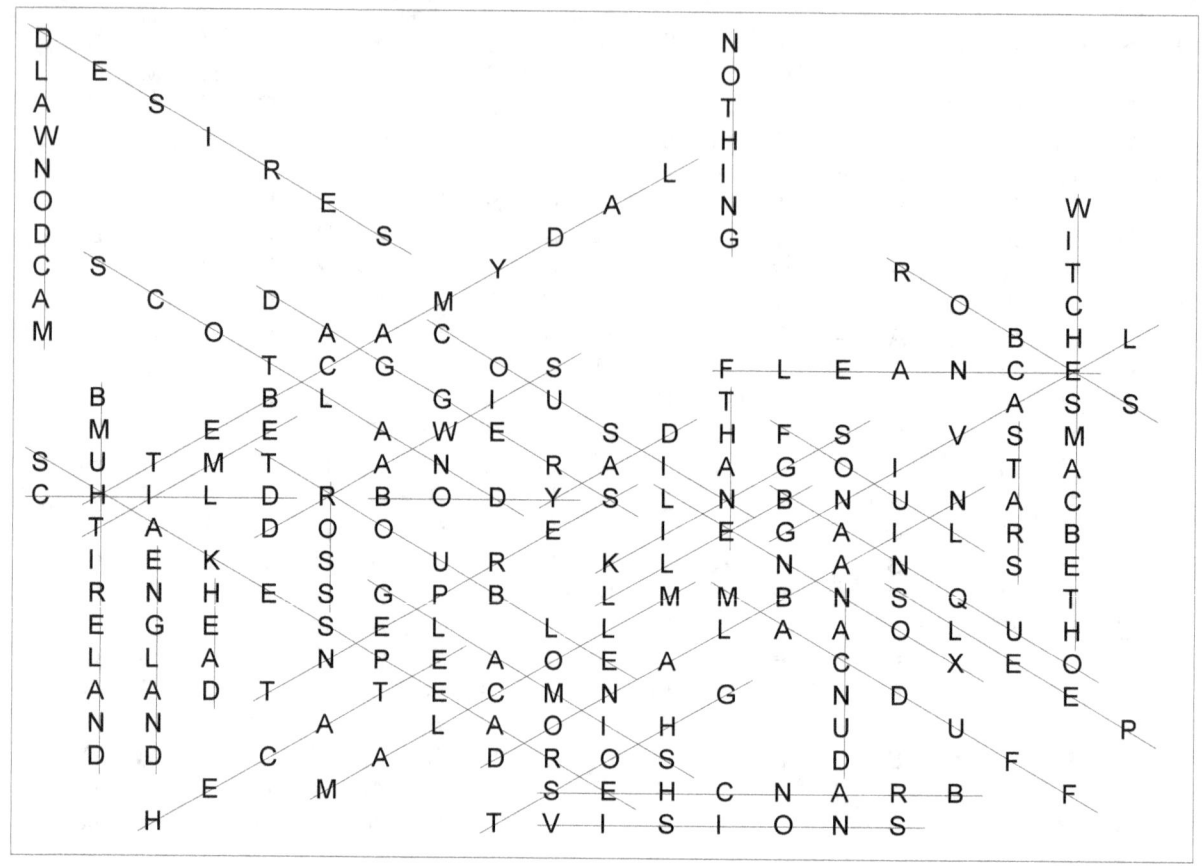

BANQUO	ENGLAND	LENNOX	SIWARD
BELL	FLEANCE	MACBETH	SLEEP
BODY	FOUL	MACDONWALD	STARS
BRANCHES	GHOST	MACDUFF	THANE
CHILD	GLAMIS	MALCOLM	THUMB
COUSIN	HEAD	NOTHING	TIME
DAGGERS	HECATE	ROBES	TROUBLE
DAY	IRELAND	ROSS	VISIONS
DESIRES	KINGS	SCOTLAND	WITCHES
DONALBAIN	LADY MACBETH	SERPENT	
DUNCAN	LEAVING	SHAKESPEARE	

Macbeth Word Search 4

```
M A C D O N W A L D L G D N A L T O C S
H C F R C K T R V R L L X H C W Z T G R
D R T J L M D P G T I K C B G W K G J K
T N R F B L A W D H Q B H B B F T K N K
F N O L V K I L C W F Q P B G L N G S B
V F U K M T R D C Q T V X M D E E X T C
Z Y B M C S J O K O F G T U L A P F A C
S G L H N D R N S M L X V H G N R R R K
M L E X D R A W I S F M E T A C E H S K
C S E X H C N Y R J W B S H C E S H Q R
X V B E N K X E W S N O F A J G A D L N
W V D U P N G M S D H H O N F K Z M A P
H F D S J G R Y A G W X U E E P T J D X
M D M C A N J E P C B H L S L C M I Y H
E O Z D C I H P M B B C P V N G A R M Q
G N Q C N V S N C V Q E W O N L C E A E
L A G M X A B O D Y A S T L X A D L C V
K L W L Y E E L Y R E H C H D M U A B H
Z B S P A L L P E R I V R B G I F N E H
K A S W L N L B I N I S U O C S F D T T
Y I B Z E J D S G S X L U K B Y P T H R
G N Y L N T E Z I F Z Q M M X E C K J Z
Z V S W N D W O W S N W Z X J H S J T Z
P N Z Q O V N B R A N C H E S G N I K R
R G C C X S N P B N V F H M K T W C N T
```

BANQUO	ENGLAND	LENNOX	SIWARD
BELL	FLEANCE	MACBETH	SLEEP
BODY	FOUL	MACDONWALD	STARS
BRANCHES	GHOST	MACDUFF	THANE
CHILD	GLAMIS	MALCOLM	THUMB
COUSIN	HEAD	NOTHING	TIME
DAGGERS	HECATE	ROBES	TROUBLE
DAY	IRELAND	ROSS	VISIONS
DESIRES	KINGS	SCOTLAND	WITCHES
DONALBAIN	LADY MACBETH	SERPENT	
DUNCAN	LEAVING	SHAKESPEARE	

Macbeth Word Search 4 Answer Key

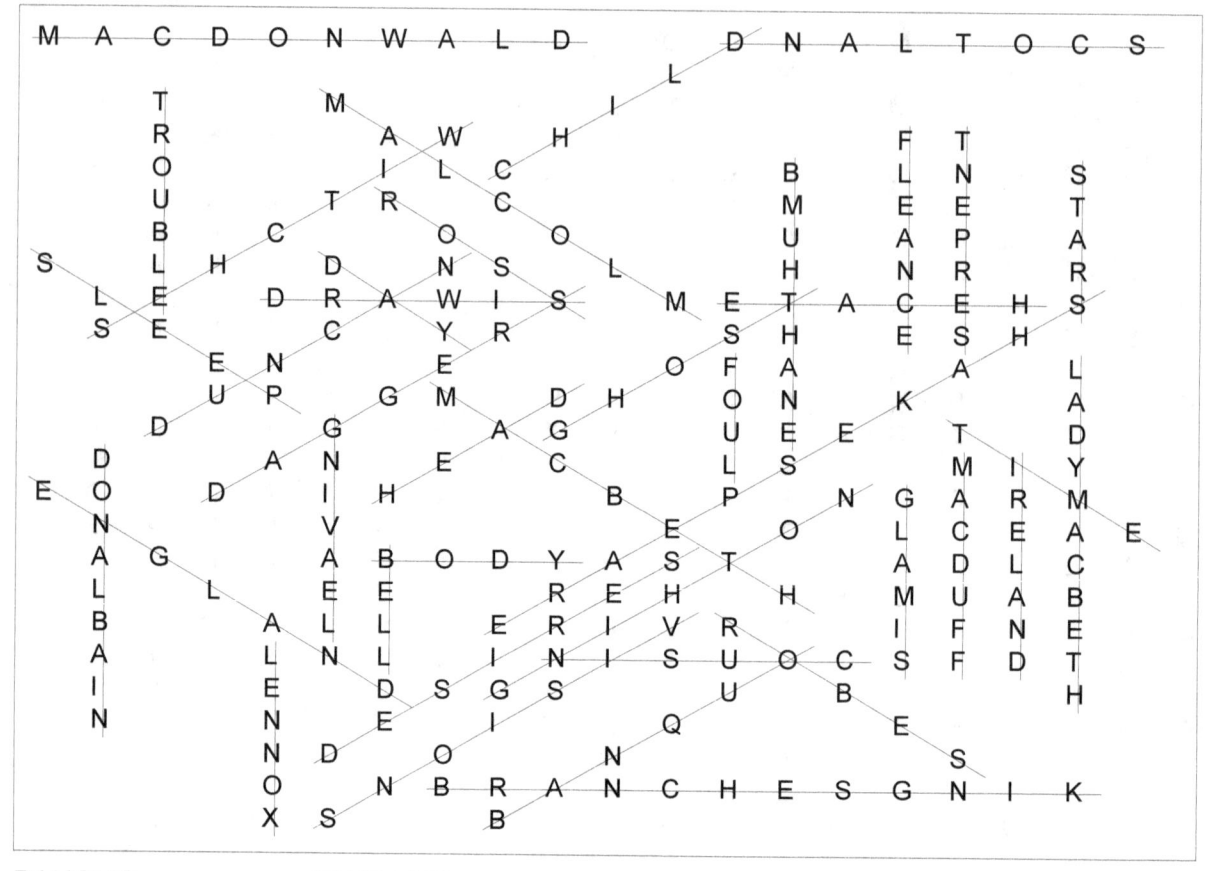

BANQUO	ENGLAND	LENNOX	SIWARD
BELL	FLEANCE	MACBETH	SLEEP
BODY	FOUL	MACDONWALD	STARS
BRANCHES	GHOST	MACDUFF	THANE
CHILD	GLAMIS	MALCOLM	THUMB
COUSIN	HEAD	NOTHING	TIME
DAGGERS	HECATE	ROBES	TROUBLE
DAY	IRELAND	ROSS	VISIONS
DESIRES	KINGS	SCOTLAND	WITCHES
DONALBAIN	LADY MACBETH	SERPENT	
DUNCAN	LEAVING	SHAKESPEARE	

Macbeth Crossword 1

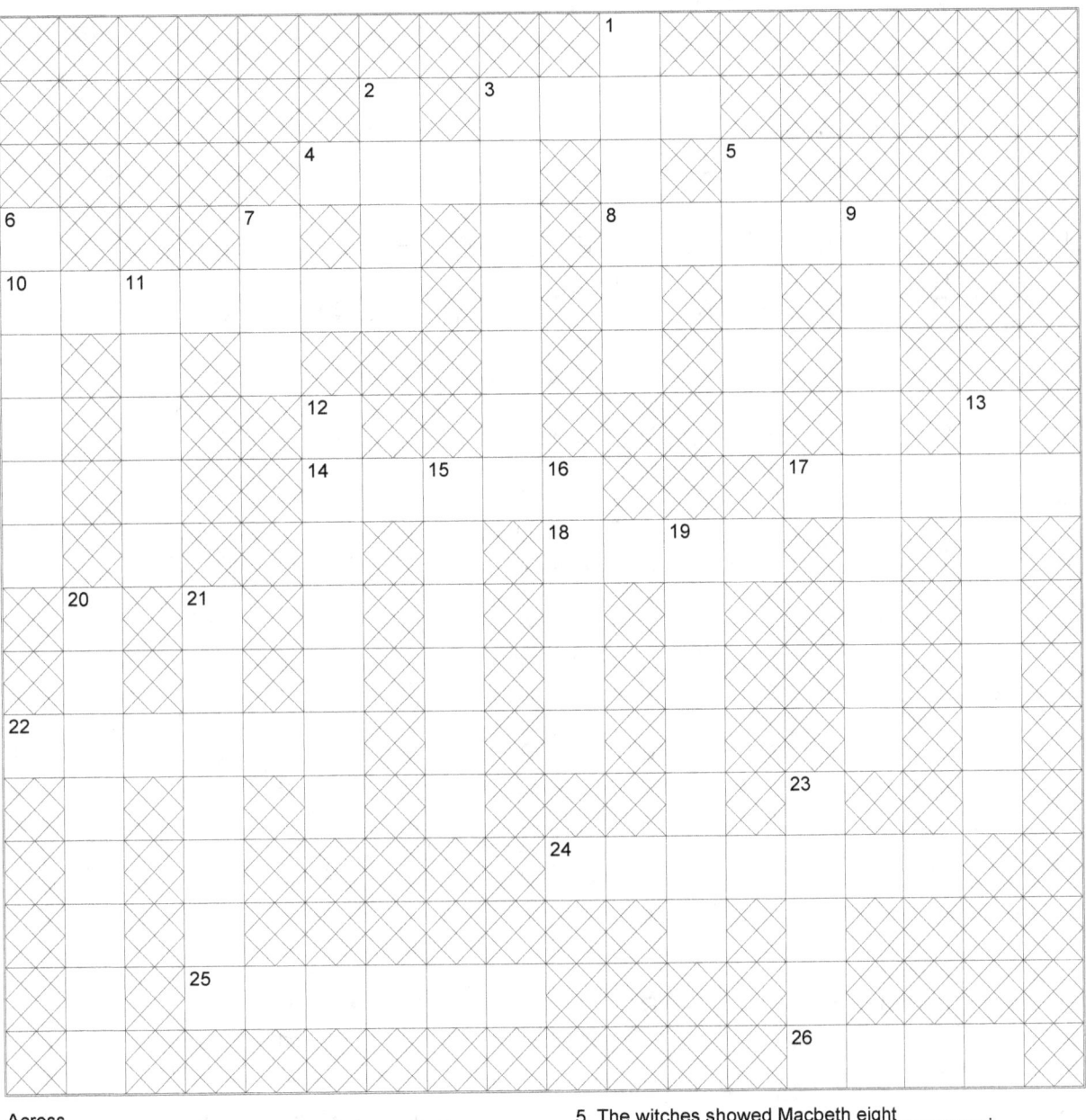

Across
3. Fair is _____, and _____ is fair.
4. Lady Macbeth's signal to Macbeth
8. The witches showed Macbeth a bloody _____.
10. Malcolm fled to this country
14. Why do you dress me in borrowed _____?
17. One thing drinking provokes
18. The _____ is free.
22. Macbeth to Duncan
24. Hecate is their queen
25. Attemtps to kill Macbeth, but he is slain
26. Macduff discovered Duncan's dead one

Down
1. King of Scotland; murdered by Macbeth
2. The witches showed Macbeth an armed _____.
3. He escapes Macbeth's murder plot, but Banquo does not
5. The witches showed Macbeth eight _____.
6. One of Duncan's noblemen
7. The night is long that never finds the _____.
9. In line for the throne after Malcolm
11. Macbeth saw Banquo's at the banquet table
12. Donalbain flees there
13. Nothing in his life/Became him like the _____ it.
15. Macbeth had him killed because he suspected Macbeth killed Duncan
16. But signs of nobleness, like _____, shall shine/On all deservers.
19. Kills Duncan to gain the throne
20. Country of which Duncan is king
21. Hecate wants the witches to give Macbeth these false impressions
23. By the pricking of my _____,/Something wicked this way comes.

Macbeth Crossword 1 Answer Key

(Crossword grid answers)

Across:
- 3. FOUL
- 4. BELL
- 8. CHILD
- 10. ENGLAND
- 14. ROBES
- 17. SLEEP
- 18. TIME
- 22. COUSIN
- 24. WITCHES
- 25. SIWARD
- 26. BODY

Down:
- 1. DUNCAN
- 2. HEAD
- 3. FLEANCE
- 5. KINGS
- 6. LENNOX
- 7. DAY
- 9. DONALBAIN
- 11. GHOST
- 12. IRELAND
- 13. LEAVING
- 15. BANQUO
- 16. STARS
- 19. MACBETH
- 20. SCOTLAND
- 21. VISIONS
- 23. THUMBS

Across
- 3. Fair is _____, and _____ is fair.
- 4. Lady Macbeth's signal to Macbeth
- 8. The witches showed Macbeth a bloody _____.
- 10. Malcolm fled to this country
- 14. Why do you dress me in borrowed _____?
- 17. One thing drinking provokes
- 18. The _____ is free.
- 22. Macbeth to Duncan
- 24. Hecate is their queen
- 25. Attemtps to kill Macbeth, but he is slain
- 26. Macduff discovered Duncan's dead one

Down
- 1. King of Scotland; murdered by Macbeth
- 2. The witches showed Macbeth an armed _____.
- 3. He escapes Macbeth's murder plot, but Banquo does not
- 5. The witches showed Macbeth eight _____.
- 6. One of Duncan's noblemen
- 7. The night is long that never finds the _____.
- 9. In line for the throne after Malcolm
- 11. Macbeth saw Banquo's at the banquet table
- 12. Donalbain flees there
- 13. Nothing in his life/Became him like the _____ it.
- 15. Macbeth had him killed because he suspected Macbeth killed Duncan
- 16. But signs of nobleness, like _____, shall shine/On all deservers.
- 19. Kills Duncan to gain the throne
- 20. Country of which Duncan is king
- 21. Hecate wants the witches to give Macbeth these false impressions
- 23. By the pricking of my _____,/Something wicked this way comes.

Macbeth Crossword 2

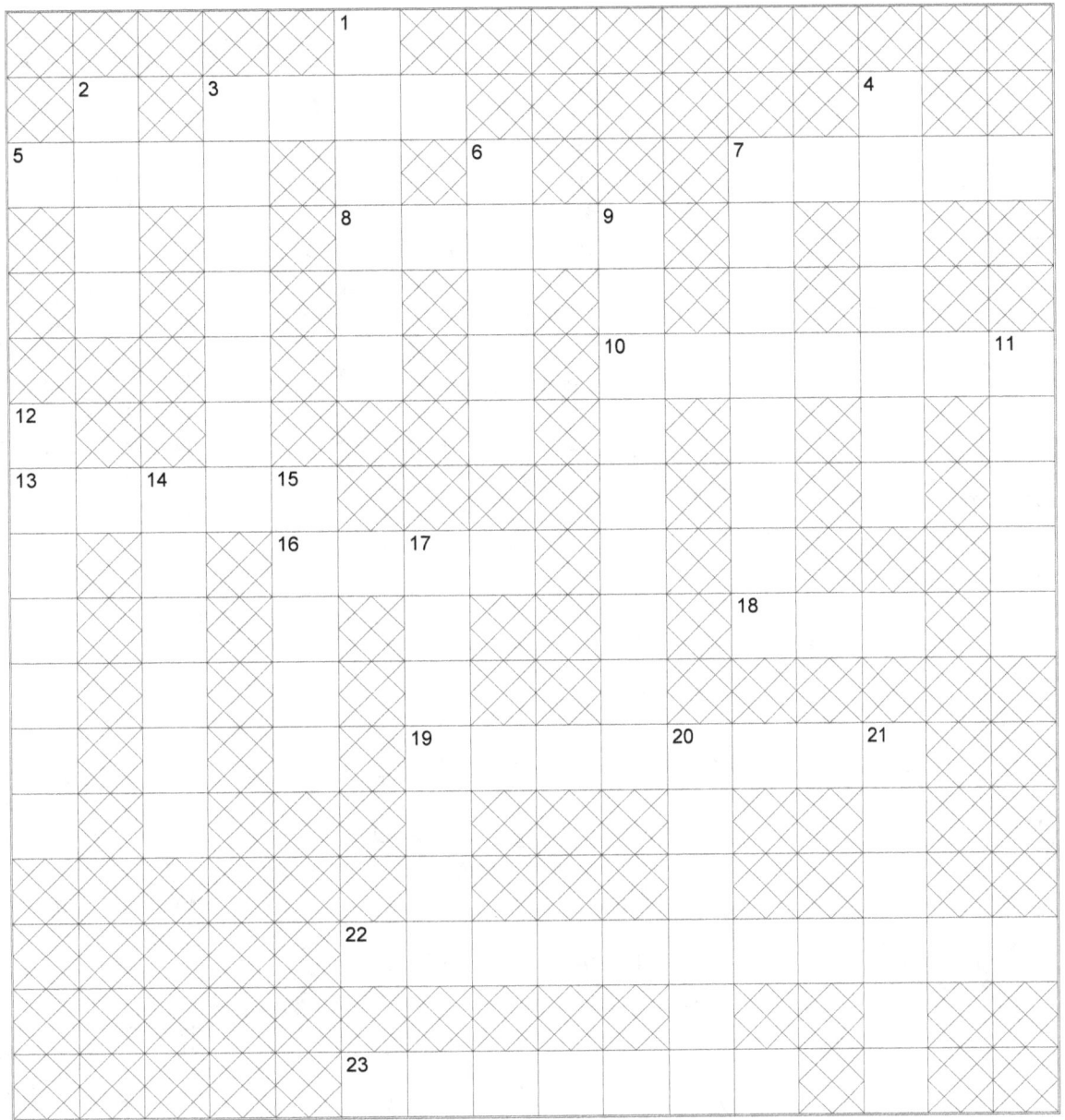

Across
3. Fair is _____, and _____ is fair.
5. Lady Macbeth's signal to Macbeth
7. One thing drinking provokes
8. The witches showed Macbeth a bloody _____.
10. It is a tale/Told by an idiot, full of sound and fury,/Signifying _____.
13. Why do you dress me in borrowed _____?
16. The _____ is free.
18. The night is long that never finds the _____.
19. Malcolm's army uses them as camouflage
22. Author
23. Hecate wants the witches to give Macbeth these false impressions

Down
1. King of Scotland; murdered by Macbeth
2. The witches showed Macbeth an armed _____.
3. He escapes Macbeth's murder plot, but Banquo does not
4. Nothing in his life/Became him like the _____ it.
6. The witches showed Macbeth eight _____.
7. Country of which Duncan is king
9. In line for the throne after Malcolm
11. Macbeth saw Banquo's at the banquet table
12. Donalbain flees there
14. Macbeth had him killed because he suspected Macbeth killed Duncan
15. But signs of nobleness, like _____, shall shine/On all deservers.
17. Kills Duncan to gain the throne
20. Macbeth to Duncan
21. Attemtps to kill Macbeth, but he is slain

Macbeth Crossword 2 Answer Key

					1 D							
	2 H		3 F	O	U	L				4 L		
5 B	E	L	L		N		6 K		7 S	L	E	E	P
	A		E		8 C	H	I	L	9 D		C	A	
	D		A		A		N		O		O	V	
			N		N		G		10 N	O	T	H	I	11 G
12 I			C				S		A		L	N		H
13 R	14 O	B	15 E	S					L		A	G		O
E			A		16 T	17 I	M	E		B		N		S
L			N		A		M			A		18 D	A	Y	T
A			Q		R		A			I				
N			U		S		19 B	R	A	N	20 C	H	E	21 S
D			O				E				O			I
							T				U			W
					22 S	H	A	K	E	S	P	E	A	R	E
											I		R
					23 V	I	S	I	O	N	S		D

Across

3. Fair is _____, and _____ is fair.
5. Lady Macbeth's signal to Macbeth
7. One thing drinking provokes
8. The witches showed Macbeth a bloody _____.
10. It is a tale/Told by an idiot, full of sound and fury,/Signifying _____.
13. Why do you dress me in borrowed _____?
16. The _____ is free.
18. The night is long that never finds the _____.
19. Malcolm's army uses them as camouflage
22. Author
23. Hecate wants the witches to give Macbeth these false impressions

Down

1. King of Scotland; murdered by Macbeth
2. The witches showed Macbeth an armed _____.
3. He escapes Macbeth's murder plot, but Banquo does not
4. Nothing in his life/Became him like the _____ it.
6. The witches showed Macbeth eight _____.
7. Country of which Duncan is king
9. In line for the throne after Malcolm
11. Macbeth saw Banquo's at the banquet table
12. Donalbain flees there
14. Macbeth had him killed because he suspected Macbeth killed Duncan
15. But signs of nobleness, like _____, shall shine/On all deservers.
17. Kills Duncan to gain the throne
20. Macbeth to Duncan
21. Attemtps to kill Macbeth, but he is slain

Macbeth Crossword 3

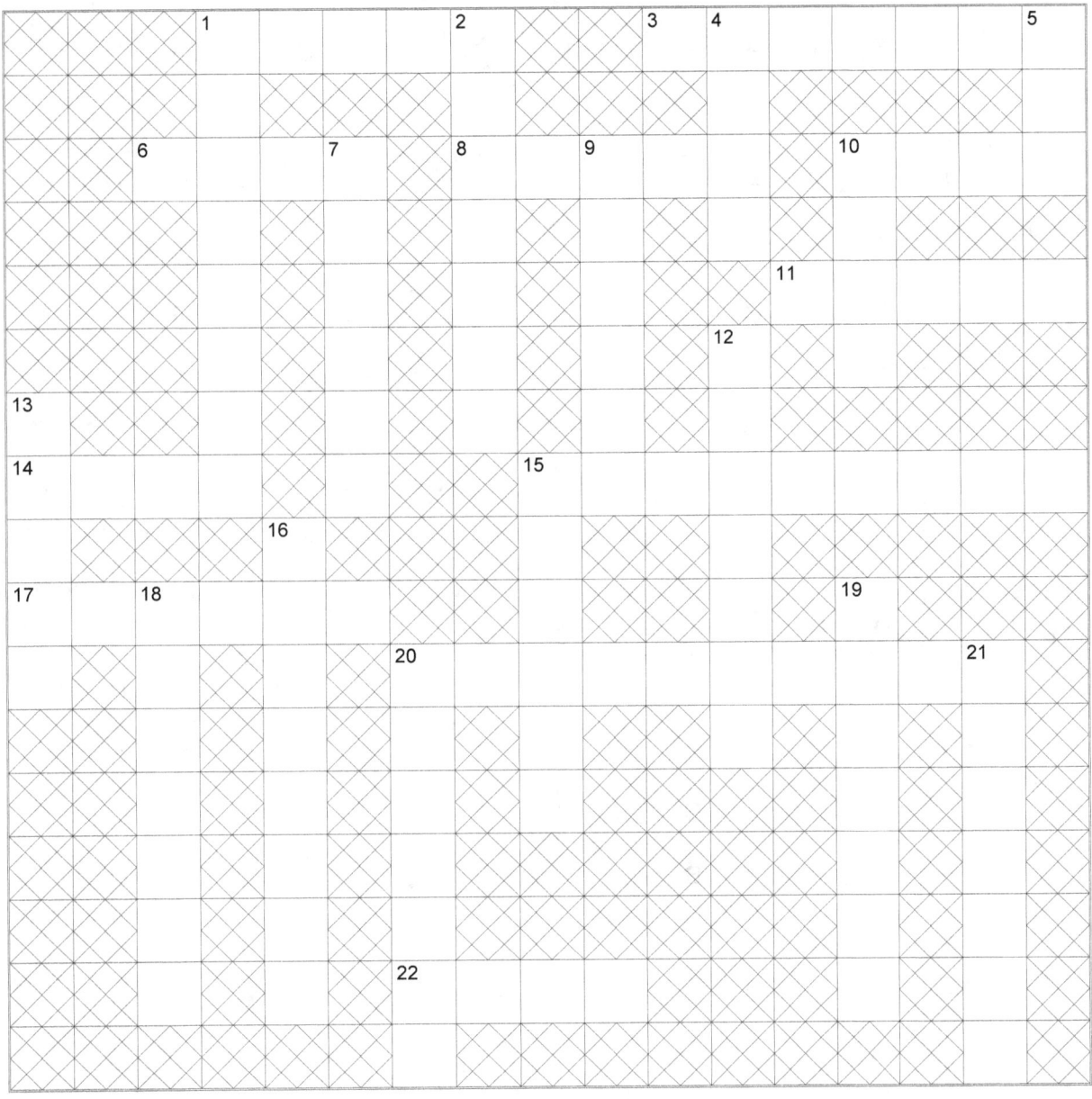

Across
1. But signs of nobleness, like _____, shall shine/On all deservers.
3. Donalbain flees there
6. Fair is _____, and _____ is fair.
8. Why do you dress me in borrowed _____?
10. Macduff discovered Duncan's dead one
11. One thing drinking provokes
14. The witches showed Macbeth an armed _____.
15. In line for the throne after Malcolm
17. Attemtps to kill Macbeth, but he is slain
20. Macbeth defeats him, which pleases Duncan
22. The _____ is free.

Down
1. Country of which Duncan is king
2. Look like the innocent flower/But be the _____ under't.
4. Messenger; he told Macduff his family was murdered
5. The night is long that never finds the _____.
7. One of Duncan's noblemen
9. Macbeth had him killed because he suspected Macbeth killed Duncan
10. Lady Macbeth's signal to Macbeth
12. Nothing in his life/Became him like the _____ it.
13. Macbeth saw Banquo's at the banquet table
15. King of Scotland; murdered by Macbeth
16. Malcolm's army uses them as camouflage
18. Hecate is their queen
19. Duncan's eldest son
20. Kills Duncan to gain the throne
21. There's _____ in men's smiles.

Macbeth Crossword 3 Answer Key

	1 S	T	A	R	2 S		3 I	4 R	E	L	A	N	5 D
		C			E			O					A
	6 F	O	7 U	8 L	9 R	O	B	E	S	10 B	O	D	Y
		T		E	P		A		S	E			
		L		N	E		N		11 S	L	E	E	P
		A		N	N		Q	12 L	L				
13 G		N		O	T		U	E					
14 H	E	A	D			15 D	O	N	A	L	B	A	I	N
O				16 B		U			V				
17 S	18 I	W	A	R	D		N			I		19 M	
T		I		A	20 M	A	C	D	O	N	W	A	L	D
		T		N	A		A			G		L		A
		C		C	C		N					C		G
		H		H	B							O		G
		E		E	E							L		E
		S		S	22 T	I	M	E				M		R
					H									S

Across
1. But signs of nobleness, like _____, shall shine/On all deservers.
3. Donalbain flees there
6. Fair is _____, and _____ is fair.
8. Why do you dress me in borrowed _____?
10. Macduff discovered Duncan's dead one
11. One thing drinking provokes
14. The witches showed Macbeth an armed _____.
15. In line for the throne after Malcolm
17. Attemtps to kill Macbeth, but he is slain
20. Macbeth defeats him, which pleases Duncan
22. The _____ is free.

Down
1. Country of which Duncan is king
2. Look like the innocent flower/But be the _____ under't.
4. Messenger; he told Macduff his family was murdered
5. The night is long that never finds the _____.
7. One of Duncan's noblemen
9. Macbeth had him killed because he suspected Macbeth killed Duncan
10. Lady Macbeth's signal to Macbeth
12. Nothing in his life/Became him like the _____ it.
13. Macbeth saw Banquo's at the banquet table
15. King of Scotland; murdered by Macbeth
16. Malcolm's army uses them as camouflage
18. Hecate is their queen
19. Duncan's eldest son
20. Kills Duncan to gain the throne
21. There's _____ in men's smiles.

Macbeth Crossword 4

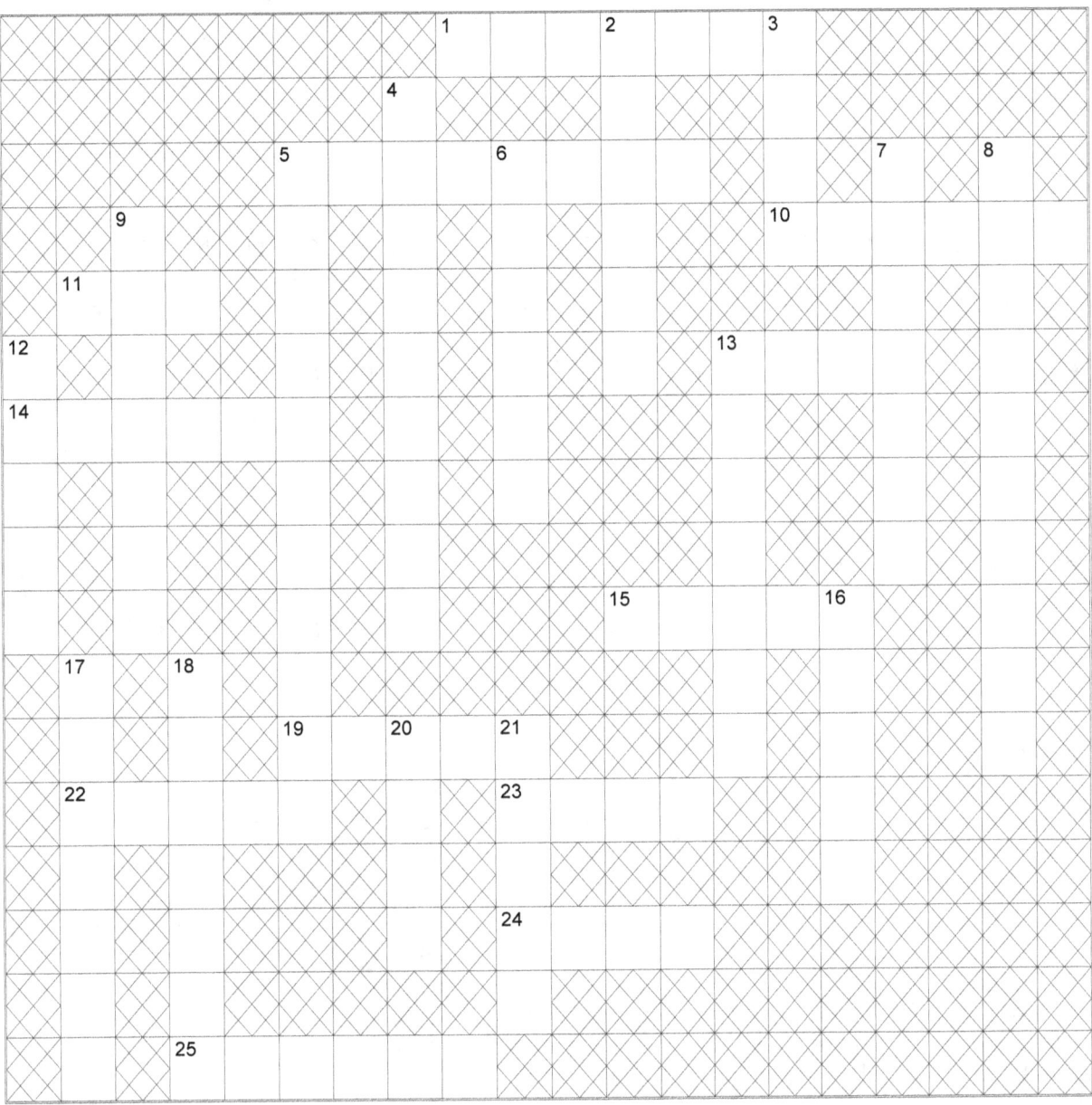

Across
1. Kills Duncan to gain the throne
5. Country of which Duncan is king
10. King of Scotland; murdered by Macbeth
11. The night is long that never finds the _____.
13. Fair is _____, and _____ is fair.
14. Queen of witches
15. The witches showed Macbeth eight _____.
19. Why do you dress me in borrowed _____?
22. _____ of Cawdor
23. The _____ is free.
24. Messenger; he told Macduff his family was murdered
25. Macbeth's original title, Thane of _____.

Down
2. Macbeth had him killed because he suspected Macbeth killed Duncan
3. The witches showed Macbeth an armed _____.
4. In line for the throne after Malcolm
5. Author
6. One of Duncan's noblemen
7. Malcolm fled to this country
8. Macbeth defeats him, which pleases Duncan
9. Duncan's eldest son
12. Macbeth saw Banquo's at the banquet table
13. He escapes Macbeth's murder plot, but Banquo does not
16. One thing drinking provokes
17. Hecate is their queen
18. Nothing in his life/Became him like the _____ it.
20. Lady Macbeth's signal to Macbeth
21. But signs of nobleness, like _____, shall shine/On all deservers.

Macbeth Crossword 4 Answer Key

Across
1. Kills Duncan to gain the throne
5. Country of which Duncan is king
10. King of Scotland; murdered by Macbeth
11. The night is long that never finds the _____.
13. Fair is _____, and _____ is fair.
14. Queen of witches
15. The witches showed Macbeth eight _____.
19. Why do you dress me in borrowed _____?
22. _____ of Cawdor
23. The _____ is free.
24. Messenger; he told Macduff his family was murdered
25. Macbeth's original title, Thane of _____.

Down
2. Macbeth had him killed because he suspected Macbeth killed Duncan
3. The witches showed Macbeth an armed _____.
4. In line for the throne after Malcolm
5. Author
6. One of Duncan's noblemen
7. Malcolm fled to this country
8. Macbeth defeats him, which pleases Duncan
9. Duncan's eldest son
12. Macbeth saw Banquo's at the banquet table
13. He escapes Macbeth's murder plot, but Banquo does not
16. One thing drinking provokes
17. Hecate is their queen
18. Nothing in his life/Became him like the _____ it.
20. Lady Macbeth's signal to Macbeth
21. But signs of nobleness, like _____, shall shine/On all deservers.

Macbeth

SERPENT	BRANCHES	NOTHING	BANQUO	DAY
SCOTLAND	CHILD	HEAD	TROUBLE	MACDUFF
THUMB	FLEANCE	FREE SPACE	THANE	BELL
GHOST	LEAVING	ROBES	MACDONWALD	VISIONS
SLEEP	TIME	STARS	COUSIN	MALCOLM

Macbeth

GLAMIS	HECATE	SHAKESPEARE	ENGLAND	WITCHES
ROSS	KINGS	DAGGERS	BODY	IRELAND
LADY MACBETH	SIWARD	FREE SPACE	FOUL	DESIRES
LENNOX	DONALBAIN	MALCOLM	COUSIN	STARS
TIME	SLEEP	VISIONS	MACDONWALD	ROBES

Macbeth

LENNOX	DUNCAN	BRANCHES	KINGS	GHOST
ROSS	VISIONS	TROUBLE	FOUL	ROBES
SLEEP	MACDUFF	FREE SPACE	CHILD	WITCHES
HECATE	SIWARD	DONALBAIN	NOTHING	ENGLAND
SCOTLAND	TIME	FLEANCE	DESIRES	MACBETH

Macbeth

HEAD	BODY	SHAKESPEARE	COUSIN	BELL
THUMB	IRELAND	SERPENT	DAGGERS	BANQUO
MALCOLM	LEAVING	FREE SPACE	MACDONWALD	GLAMIS
DAY	LADY MACBETH	MACBETH	DESIRES	FLEANCE
TIME	SCOTLAND	ENGLAND	NOTHING	DONALBAIN

Macbeth

BODY	BELL	HECATE	FOUL	THUMB
SERPENT	TROUBLE	GLAMIS	STARS	SLEEP
DUNCAN	NOTHING	FREE SPACE	LADY MACBETH	BANQUO
ENGLAND	SHAKESPEARE	KINGS	DAY	TIME
MACDUFF	MACDONWALD	MALCOLM	DONALBAIN	SCOTLAND

Macbeth

CHILD	THANE	VISIONS	WITCHES	MACBETH
DAGGERS	FLEANCE	LEAVING	HEAD	ROSS
SIWARD	ROBES	FREE SPACE	DESIRES	GHOST
COUSIN	LENNOX	SCOTLAND	DONALBAIN	MALCOLM
MACDONWALD	MACDUFF	TIME	DAY	KINGS

Macbeth

GLAMIS	TROUBLE	MACDONWALD	THUMB	LEAVING
DONALBAIN	SLEEP	HECATE	WITCHES	DAGGERS
HEAD	LADY MACBETH	FREE SPACE	FLEANCE	BANQUO
COUSIN	IRELAND	LENNOX	ROBES	SERPENT
BRANCHES	VISIONS	NOTHING	GHOST	TIME

Macbeth

CHILD	DAY	MALCOLM	SCOTLAND	THANE
BODY	BELL	MACDUFF	MACBETH	DESIRES
STARS	SHAKESPEARE	FREE SPACE	SIWARD	DUNCAN
KINGS	FOUL	TIME	GHOST	NOTHING
VISIONS	BRANCHES	SERPENT	ROBES	LENNOX

Macbeth

MACDUFF	LADY MACBETH	BANQUO	HECATE	LEAVING
DESIRES	SLEEP	MACBETH	DAGGERS	COUSIN
DUNCAN	IRELAND	FREE SPACE	KINGS	DONALBAIN
BRANCHES	BODY	GLAMIS	MALCOLM	ROSS
DAY	THANE	THUMB	SIWARD	TIME

Macbeth

SERPENT	HEAD	WITCHES	STARS	CHILD
ENGLAND	VISIONS	TROUBLE	BELL	FLEANCE
MACDONWALD	SHAKESPEARE	FREE SPACE	NOTHING	GHOST
LENNOX	FOUL	TIME	SIWARD	THUMB
THANE	DAY	ROSS	MALCOLM	GLAMIS

Macbeth

MACDUFF	SCOTLAND	BANQUO	ENGLAND	DAGGERS
BELL	LENNOX	WITCHES	BRANCHES	ROBES
LADY MACBETH	DAY	FREE SPACE	BODY	GLAMIS
THUMB	TROUBLE	FOUL	COUSIN	FLEANCE
SHAKESPEARE	MALCOLM	SLEEP	KINGS	DUNCAN

Macbeth

DONALBAIN	SERPENT	THANE	STARS	TIME
NOTHING	VISIONS	ROSS	MACBETH	IRELAND
HEAD	SIWARD	FREE SPACE	CHILD	LEAVING
DESIRES	MACDONWALD	DUNCAN	KINGS	SLEEP
MALCOLM	SHAKESPEARE	FLEANCE	COUSIN	FOUL

Macbeth

TIME	FLEANCE	DUNCAN	STARS	THUMB
BODY	SLEEP	ROSS	SHAKESPEARE	LEAVING
SERPENT	FOUL	FREE SPACE	DESIRES	TROUBLE
DAY	BRANCHES	THANE	VISIONS	DAGGERS
ROBES	LADY MACBETH	SCOTLAND	MACDUFF	CHILD

Macbeth

LENNOX	WITCHES	ENGLAND	MALCOLM	COUSIN
GHOST	KINGS	HEAD	BANQUO	MACDONWALD
BELL	IRELAND	FREE SPACE	GLAMIS	NOTHING
MACBETH	DONALBAIN	CHILD	MACDUFF	SCOTLAND
LADY MACBETH	ROBES	DAGGERS	VISIONS	THANE

Macbeth

THUMB	TIME	BELL	DESIRES	ROBES
DAGGERS	VISIONS	MACDONWALD	LENNOX	ENGLAND
CHILD	FOUL	FREE SPACE	SIWARD	IRELAND
WITCHES	DONALBAIN	BODY	SHAKESPEARE	HEAD
STARS	DUNCAN	GHOST	SERPENT	FLEANCE

Macbeth

MACBETH	HECATE	BRANCHES	THANE	TROUBLE
ROSS	GLAMIS	MACDUFF	LEAVING	KINGS
MALCOLM	SLEEP	FREE SPACE	SCOTLAND	BANQUO
NOTHING	COUSIN	FLEANCE	SERPENT	GHOST
DUNCAN	STARS	HEAD	SHAKESPEARE	BODY

Macbeth

ENGLAND	HECATE	LENNOX	COUSIN	LADY MACBETH
MACDONWALD	SHAKESPEARE	WITCHES	IRELAND	DESIRES
TROUBLE	MACDUFF	FREE SPACE	ROBES	KINGS
FLEANCE	SLEEP	SIWARD	SCOTLAND	GHOST
BELL	BRANCHES	FOUL	DAY	CHILD

Macbeth

HEAD	DUNCAN	VISIONS	THUMB	GLAMIS
BANQUO	ROSS	MALCOLM	BODY	NOTHING
DONALBAIN	SERPENT	FREE SPACE	STARS	THANE
TIME	LEAVING	CHILD	DAY	FOUL
BRANCHES	BELL	GHOST	SCOTLAND	SIWARD

Macbeth

DONALBAIN	NOTHING	LADY MACBETH	TIME	THUMB
DUNCAN	ROBES	MACBETH	MACDONWALD	VISIONS
IRELAND	WITCHES	FREE SPACE	MACDUFF	GHOST
HEAD	FLEANCE	HECATE	DESIRES	DAGGERS
BELL	SERPENT	THANE	SHAKESPEARE	FOUL

Macbeth

DAY	GLAMIS	STARS	BANQUO	CHILD
BODY	ENGLAND	SCOTLAND	BRANCHES	KINGS
TROUBLE	SLEEP	FREE SPACE	LEAVING	LENNOX
COUSIN	MALCOLM	FOUL	SHAKESPEARE	THANE
SERPENT	BELL	DAGGERS	DESIRES	HECATE

Macbeth

MACDUFF	MACDONWALD	SLEEP	COUSIN	HECATE
LENNOX	WITCHES	BELL	DESIRES	SERPENT
SCOTLAND	NOTHING	FREE SPACE	MACBETH	LEAVING
SIWARD	SHAKESPEARE	FOUL	FLEANCE	DUNCAN
BRANCHES	TROUBLE	ROSS	VISIONS	IRELAND

Macbeth

THUMB	TIME	THANE	LADY MACBETH	ENGLAND
DAGGERS	ROBES	HEAD	BANQUO	DAY
GHOST	DONALBAIN	FREE SPACE	STARS	BODY
KINGS	MALCOLM	IRELAND	VISIONS	ROSS
TROUBLE	BRANCHES	DUNCAN	FLEANCE	FOUL

Macbeth

DESIRES	MACBETH	SIWARD	THANE	GHOST
BELL	BODY	FLEANCE	BANQUO	MALCOLM
DAGGERS	GLAMIS	FREE SPACE	COUSIN	SLEEP
ROBES	HECATE	TROUBLE	BRANCHES	STARS
SERPENT	KINGS	LADY MACBETH	DUNCAN	IRELAND

Macbeth

SHAKESPEARE	SCOTLAND	MACDONWALD	NOTHING	LENNOX
HEAD	LEAVING	THUMB	FOUL	DONALBAIN
ENGLAND	ROSS	FREE SPACE	CHILD	VISIONS
DAY	MACDUFF	IRELAND	DUNCAN	LADY MACBETH
KINGS	SERPENT	STARS	BRANCHES	TROUBLE

Macbeth

VISIONS	ENGLAND	LENNOX	SERPENT	BELL
CHILD	GLAMIS	GHOST	DONALBAIN	DAY
ROSS	BRANCHES	FREE SPACE	TIME	MALCOLM
BANQUO	SIWARD	SCOTLAND	COUSIN	IRELAND
STARS	THANE	NOTHING	LEAVING	LADY MACBETH

Macbeth

THUMB	DUNCAN	HECATE	ROBES	DAGGERS
MACDONWALD	SHAKESPEARE	MACDUFF	WITCHES	MACBETH
TROUBLE	HEAD	FREE SPACE	FLEANCE	FOUL
KINGS	SLEEP	LADY MACBETH	LEAVING	NOTHING
THANE	STARS	IRELAND	COUSIN	SCOTLAND

Macbeth

SIWARD	SHAKESPEARE	VISIONS	BANQUO	SERPENT
MALCOLM	GHOST	ROSS	IRELAND	HECATE
TIME	KINGS	FREE SPACE	DONALBAIN	THANE
FOUL	DESIRES	NOTHING	MACBETH	TROUBLE
THUMB	DUNCAN	GLAMIS	DAY	STARS

Macbeth

BELL	WITCHES	BRANCHES	LENNOX	MACDONWALD
BODY	COUSIN	LADY MACBETH	LEAVING	DAGGERS
CHILD	SCOTLAND	FREE SPACE	ROBES	ENGLAND
SLEEP	FLEANCE	STARS	DAY	GLAMIS
DUNCAN	THUMB	TROUBLE	MACBETH	NOTHING

Macbeth

STARS	NOTHING	MALCOLM	LENNOX	COUSIN
DUNCAN	MACDONWALD	DAGGERS	BELL	VISIONS
SERPENT	CHILD	FREE SPACE	DAY	SLEEP
HEAD	IRELAND	THANE	SCOTLAND	WITCHES
MACBETH	DONALBAIN	SHAKESPEARE	BODY	ENGLAND

Macbeth

KINGS	ROBES	MACDUFF	GLAMIS	DESIRES
TIME	FLEANCE	LEAVING	FOUL	LADY MACBETH
HECATE	SIWARD	FREE SPACE	BRANCHES	ROSS
BANQUO	TROUBLE	ENGLAND	BODY	SHAKESPEARE
DONALBAIN	MACBETH	WITCHES	SCOTLAND	THANE

Macbeth

LEAVING	BELL	HEAD	IRELAND	DUNCAN
DAGGERS	DAY	MALCOLM	THUMB	LADY MACBETH
TROUBLE	COUSIN	FREE SPACE	KINGS	DONALBAIN
LENNOX	BODY	CHILD	NOTHING	GLAMIS
HECATE	TIME	SERPENT	SIWARD	VISIONS

Macbeth

SCOTLAND	SHAKESPEARE	MACBETH	MACDUFF	SLEEP
GHOST	BANQUO	FLEANCE	ENGLAND	MACDONWALD
WITCHES	FOUL	FREE SPACE	THANE	STARS
DESIRES	ROBES	VISIONS	SIWARD	SERPENT
TIME	HECATE	GLAMIS	NOTHING	CHILD

Macbeth Vocabulary Word List

No.	Word	Clue/Definition
1.	AGUE	A chill or fit of shivering
2.	APPALL	To fill with dismay
3.	APPEASE	To bring peace
4.	AVARICIOUS	Immoderate desire for wealth
5.	BEGUILE	To pass (time) pleasantly
6.	BIDES	To wait
7.	BRANDISHED	To wave or flourish
8.	CALDRON	A large vessel
9.	CAROUSING	Drunken merrymaking
10.	CENSURES	Harsh criticisms
11.	CHASTISE	To punish
12.	CLEAVE	To adhere, cling or stick fast
13.	CORPORAL	Of or relating to the body
14.	COURIERS	A messenger
15.	DEFTLY	Quickly and skillfully
16.	DIMINUTIVE	Extremely small in size
17.	EQUIVOCATES	To avoid making an explicit statement
18.	HARBINGER	One that indicates what is to come
19.	HOMAGE	Special honor expressed publicly
20.	INTEGRITY	Steadfast adherence to a strict moral code
21.	INTERDICTION	To forbid authoritatively
22.	MALICE	Extreme ill will or spite
23.	MINION	An obsequious follower
24.	MUSE	To consider
25.	PALPABLE	Easily perceived
26.	PARRICIDE	The murdering of one's father, mother or relative
27.	PERNICIOUS	Evil; wicked
28.	PURGED	To free from impurities
29.	SCRUPLES	To hesitate as a result of conscience
30.	SUBORNED	Induced to commit an unlawful act
31.	VIZARDS	Mask

Macbeth Vocabulary Fill In The Blanks 1

_____ 1. To wait
_____ 2. To adhere, cling or stick fast
_____ 3. Easily perceived
_____ 4. Extreme ill will or spite
_____ 5. To pass (time) pleasantly
_____ 6. To wave or flourish
_____ 7. To hesitate as a result of conscience
_____ 8. Special honor expressed publicly
_____ 9. To fill with dismay
_____ 10. Harsh criticisms
_____ 11. An obsequious follower
_____ 12. To consider
_____ 13. Drunken merrymaking
_____ 14. To free from impurities
_____ 15. Of or relating to the body
_____ 16. To forbid authoritatively
_____ 17. Extremely small in size
_____ 18. The murdering of one's father, mother or relative
_____ 19. A chill or fit of shivering
_____ 20. Mask

Macbeth Vocabulary Fill In The Blanks 1 Answer Key

BIDES	1. To wait
CLEAVE	2. To adhere, cling or stick fast
PALPABLE	3. Easily perceived
MALICE	4. Extreme ill will or spite
BEGUILE	5. To pass (time) pleasantly
BRANDISHED	6. To wave or flourish
SCRUPLES	7. To hesitate as a result of conscience
HOMAGE	8. Special honor expressed publicly
APPALL	9. To fill with dismay
CENSURES	10. Harsh criticisms
MINION	11. An obsequious follower
MUSE	12. To consider
CAROUSING	13. Drunken merrymaking
PURGED	14. To free from impurities
CORPORAL	15. Of or relating to the body
INTERDICTION	16. To forbid authoritatively
DIMINUTIVE	17. Extremely small in size
PARRICIDE	18. The murdering of one's father, mother or relative
AGUE	19. A chill or fit of shivering
VIZARDS	20. Mask

Macbeth Vocabulary Fill In The Blanks 2

_____   1. To pass (time) pleasantly
_____   2. One that indicates what is to come
_____   3. To avoid making an explicit statement
_____   4. An obsequious follower
_____   5. Easily perceived
_____   6. To fill with dismay
_____   7. Immoderate desire for wealth
_____   8. To free from impurities
_____   9. Induced to commit an unlawful act
_____   10. Of or relating to the body
_____   11. To adhere, cling or stick fast
_____   12. Extreme ill will or spite
_____   13. Drunken merrymaking
_____   14. To consider
_____   15. To punish
_____   16. To wait
_____   17. To wave or flourish
_____   18. Quickly and skillfully
_____   19. A large vessel
_____   20. Harsh criticisms

Macbeth Vocabulary Fill In The Blanks 2 Answer Key

BEGUILE	1. To pass (time) pleasantly
HARBINGER	2. One that indicates what is to come
EQUIVOCATES	3. To avoid making an explicit statement
MINION	4. An obsequious follower
PALPABLE	5. Easily perceived
APPALL	6. To fill with dismay
AVARICIOUS	7. Immoderate desire for wealth
PURGED	8. To free from impurities
SUBORNED	9. Induced to commit an unlawful act
CORPORAL	10. Of or relating to the body
CLEAVE	11. To adhere, cling or stick fast
MALICE	12. Extreme ill will or spite
CAROUSING	13. Drunken merrymaking
MUSE	14. To consider
CHASTISE	15. To punish
BIDES	16. To wait
BRANDISHED	17. To wave or flourish
DEFTLY	18. Quickly and skillfully
CALDRON	19. A large vessel
CENSURES	20. Harsh criticisms

Macbeth Vocabulary Fill In The Blanks 3

_____   1. Extreme ill will or spite

_____   2. Special honor expressed publicly

_____   3. To punish

_____   4. To hesitate as a result of conscience

_____   5. A messenger

_____   6. A chill or fit of shivering

_____   7. Drunken merrymaking

_____   8. To forbid authoritatively

_____   9. Easily perceived

_____   10. To wait

_____   11. Immoderate desire for wealth

_____   12. Steadfast adherence to a strict moral code

_____   13. To pass (time) pleasantly

_____   14. Harsh criticisms

_____   15. Induced to commit an unlawful act

_____   16. To avoid making an explicit statement

_____   17. To fill with dismay

_____   18. One that indicates what is to come

_____   19. To consider

_____   20. An obsequious follower

Macbeth Vocabulary Fill In The Blanks 3 Answer Key

MALICE	1. Extreme ill will or spite
HOMAGE	2. Special honor expressed publicly
CHASTISE	3. To punish
SCRUPLES	4. To hesitate as a result of conscience
COURIERS	5. A messenger
AGUE	6. A chill or fit of shivering
CAROUSING	7. Drunken merrymaking
INTERDICTION	8. To forbid authoritatively
PALPABLE	9. Easily perceived
BIDES	10. To wait
AVARICIOUS	11. Immoderate desire for wealth
INTEGRITY	12. Steadfast adherence to a strict moral code
BEGUILE	13. To pass (time) pleasantly
CENSURES	14. Harsh criticisms
SUBORNED	15. Induced to commit an unlawful act
EQUIVOCATES	16. To avoid making an explicit statement
APPALL	17. To fill with dismay
HARBINGER	18. One that indicates what is to come
MUSE	19. To consider
MINION	20. An obsequious follower

Copyrighted

Macbeth Vocabulary Fill In The Blanks 4

_____ 1. An obsequious follower

_____ 2. Steadfast adherence to a strict moral code

_____ 3. Quickly and skillfully

_____ 4. Of or relating to the body

_____ 5. Evil; wicked

_____ 6. To bring peace

_____ 7. To wait

_____ 8. Extremely small in size

_____ 9. Harsh criticisms

_____ 10. To pass (time) pleasantly

_____ 11. To consider

_____ 12. Drunken merrymaking

_____ 13. To adhere, cling or stick fast

_____ 14. To fill with dismay

_____ 15. One that indicates what is to come

_____ 16. To hesitate as a result of conscience

_____ 17. To wave or flourish

_____ 18. Immoderate desire for wealth

_____ 19. Special honor expressed publicly

_____ 20. A messenger

Macbeth Vocabulary Fill In The Blanks 4 Answer Key

MINION	1. An obsequious follower
INTEGRITY	2. Steadfast adherence to a strict moral code
DEFTLY	3. Quickly and skillfully
CORPORAL	4. Of or relating to the body
PERNICIOUS	5. Evil; wicked
APPEASE	6. To bring peace
BIDES	7. To wait
DIMINUTIVE	8. Extremely small in size
CENSURES	9. Harsh criticisms
BEGUILE	10. To pass (time) pleasantly
MUSE	11. To consider
CAROUSING	12. Drunken merrymaking
CLEAVE	13. To adhere, cling or stick fast
APPALL	14. To fill with dismay
HARBINGER	15. One that indicates what is to come
SCRUPLES	16. To hesitate as a result of conscience
BRANDISHED	17. To wave or flourish
AVARICIOUS	18. Immoderate desire for wealth
HOMAGE	19. Special honor expressed publicly
COURIERS	20. A messenger

Macbeth Vocabulary Matching 1

___ 1. INTEGRITY   A. To consider
___ 2. APPEASE   B. Quickly and skillfully
___ 3. CORPORAL   C. One that indicates what is to come
___ 4. HARBINGER   D. Immoderate desire for wealth
___ 5. PARRICIDE   E. Of or relating to the body
___ 6. MUSE   F. The murdering of one's father, mother or relative
___ 7. MALICE   G. Easily perceived
___ 8. HOMAGE   H. Drunken merrymaking
___ 9. MINION   I. A chill or fit of shivering
___10. CALDRON   J. Special honor expressed publicly
___11. EQUIVOCATES   K. Extremely small in size
___12. BRANDISHED   L. To punish
___13. INTERDICTION   M. To fill with dismay
___14. SCRUPLES   N. Extreme ill will or spite
___15. CAROUSING   O. An obsequious follower
___16. BEGUILE   P. To bring peace
___17. PERNICIOUS   Q. Evil; wicked
___18. CENSURES   R. To wave or flourish
___19. DEFTLY   S. To pass (time) pleasantly
___20. PALPABLE   T. To forbid authoritatively
___21. DIMINUTIVE   U. Steadfast adherence to a strict moral code
___22. AGUE   V. To avoid making an explicit statement
___23. APPALL   W. Harsh criticisms
___24. CHASTISE   X. A large vessel
___25. AVARICIOUS   Y. To hesitate as a result of conscience

Macbeth Vocabulary Matching 1 Answer Key

U - 1. INTEGRITY   A. To consider
P - 2. APPEASE   B. Quickly and skillfully
E - 3. CORPORAL   C. One that indicates what is to come
C - 4. HARBINGER   D. Immoderate desire for wealth
F - 5. PARRICIDE   E. Of or relating to the body
A - 6. MUSE   F. The murdering of one's father, mother or relative
N - 7. MALICE   G. Easily perceived
J - 8. HOMAGE   H. Drunken merrymaking
O - 9. MINION   I. A chill or fit of shivering
X - 10. CALDRON   J. Special honor expressed publicly
V - 11. EQUIVOCATES   K. Extremely small in size
R - 12. BRANDISHED   L. To punish
T - 13. INTERDICTION   M. To fill with dismay
Y - 14. SCRUPLES   N. Extreme ill will or spite
H - 15. CAROUSING   O. An obsequious follower
S - 16. BEGUILE   P. To bring peace
Q - 17. PERNICIOUS   Q. Evil; wicked
W - 18. CENSURES   R. To wave or flourish
B - 19. DEFTLY   S. To pass (time) pleasantly
G - 20. PALPABLE   T. To forbid authoritatively
K - 21. DIMINUTIVE   U. Steadfast adherence to a strict moral code
I - 22. AGUE   V. To avoid making an explicit statement
M - 23. APPALL   W. Harsh criticisms
L - 24. CHASTISE   X. A large vessel
D - 25. AVARICIOUS   Y. To hesitate as a result of conscience

Macbeth Vocabulary Matching 2

___ 1. VIZARDS   A. Steadfast adherence to a strict moral code
___ 2. AVARICIOUS   B. To avoid making an explicit statement
___ 3. PERNICIOUS   C. To forbid authoritatively
___ 4. EQUIVOCATES   D. To hesitate as a result of conscience
___ 5. APPALL   E. To pass (time) pleasantly
___ 6. CORPORAL   F. Mask
___ 7. CENSURES   G. To wait
___ 8. APPEASE   H. To punish
___ 9. BRANDISHED   I. Evil; wicked
___ 10. CAROUSING   J. Of or relating to the body
___ 11. SCRUPLES   K. Immoderate desire for wealth
___ 12. PURGED   L. To wave or flourish
___ 13. INTEGRITY   M. Induced to commit an unlawful act
___ 14. INTERDICTION   N. To adhere, cling or stick fast
___ 15. HARBINGER   O. One that indicates what is to come
___ 16. MUSE   P. Special honor expressed publicly
___ 17. HOMAGE   Q. To consider
___ 18. BEGUILE   R. To fill with dismay
___ 19. CLEAVE   S. Extreme ill will or spite
___ 20. DIMINUTIVE   T. To free from impurities
___ 21. MALICE   U. Harsh criticisms
___ 22. BIDES   V. Extremely small in size
___ 23. COURIERS   W. A messenger
___ 24. SUBORNED   X. To bring peace
___ 25. CHASTISE   Y. Drunken merrymaking

Macbeth Vocabulary Matching 2 Answer Key

F - 1.	VIZARDS	A.	Steadfast adherence to a strict moral code
K - 2.	AVARICIOUS	B.	To avoid making an explicit statement
I - 3.	PERNICIOUS	C.	To forbid authoritatively
B - 4.	EQUIVOCATES	D.	To hesitate as a result of conscience
R - 5.	APPALL	E.	To pass (time) pleasantly
J - 6.	CORPORAL	F.	Mask
U - 7.	CENSURES	G.	To wait
X - 8.	APPEASE	H.	To punish
L - 9.	BRANDISHED	I.	Evil; wicked
Y - 10.	CAROUSING	J.	Of or relating to the body
D - 11.	SCRUPLES	K.	Immoderate desire for wealth
T - 12.	PURGED	L.	To wave or flourish
A - 13.	INTEGRITY	M.	Induced to commit an unlawful act
C - 14.	INTERDICTION	N.	To adhere, cling or stick fast
O - 15.	HARBINGER	O.	One that indicates what is to come
Q - 16.	MUSE	P.	Special honor expressed publicly
P - 17.	HOMAGE	Q.	To consider
E - 18.	BEGUILE	R.	To fill with dismay
N - 19.	CLEAVE	S.	Extreme ill will or spite
V - 20.	DIMINUTIVE	T.	To free from impurities
S - 21.	MALICE	U.	Harsh criticisms
G - 22.	BIDES	V.	Extremely small in size
W - 23.	COURIERS	W.	A messenger
M - 24.	SUBORNED	X.	To bring peace
H - 25.	CHASTISE	Y.	Drunken merrymaking

Macbeth Vocabulary Matching 3

___ 1. DEFTLY A. Of or relating to the body
___ 2. BIDES B. Drunken merrymaking
___ 3. CALDRON C. To avoid making an explicit statement
___ 4. PERNICIOUS D. A chill or fit of shivering
___ 5. APPALL E. To pass (time) pleasantly
___ 6. CHASTISE F. To adhere, cling or stick fast
___ 7. PALPABLE G. To forbid authoritatively
___ 8. CORPORAL H. Special honor expressed publicly
___ 9. AVARICIOUS I. To consider
___10. INTEGRITY J. Induced to commit an unlawful act
___11. SUBORNED K. An obsequious follower
___12. MINION L. To fill with dismay
___13. AGUE M. A large vessel
___14. SCRUPLES N. Steadfast adherence to a strict moral code
___15. APPEASE O. To bring peace
___16. HOMAGE P. To free from impurities
___17. CAROUSING Q. Quickly and skillfully
___18. MUSE R. To hesitate as a result of conscience
___19. BEGUILE S. To wait
___20. CLEAVE T. To punish
___21. HARBINGER U. Easily perceived
___22. COURIERS V. One that indicates what is to come
___23. PURGED W. Evil; wicked
___24. EQUIVOCATES X. Immoderate desire for wealth
___25. INTERDICTION Y. A messenger

Macbeth Vocabulary Matching 3 Answer Key

Q - 1.	DEFTLY	A.	Of or relating to the body
S - 2.	BIDES	B.	Drunken merrymaking
M - 3.	CALDRON	C.	To avoid making an explicit statement
W - 4.	PERNICIOUS	D.	A chill or fit of shivering
L - 5.	APPALL	E.	To pass (time) pleasantly
T - 6.	CHASTISE	F.	To adhere, cling or stick fast
U - 7.	PALPABLE	G.	To forbid authoritatively
A - 8.	CORPORAL	H.	Special honor expressed publicly
X - 9.	AVARICIOUS	I.	To consider
N - 10.	INTEGRITY	J.	Induced to commit an unlawful act
J - 11.	SUBORNED	K.	An obsequious follower
K - 12.	MINION	L.	To fill with dismay
D - 13.	AGUE	M.	A large vessel
R - 14.	SCRUPLES	N.	Steadfast adherence to a strict moral code
O - 15.	APPEASE	O.	To bring peace
H - 16.	HOMAGE	P.	To free from impurities
B - 17.	CAROUSING	Q.	Quickly and skillfully
I - 18.	MUSE	R.	To hesitate as a result of conscience
E - 19.	BEGUILE	S.	To wait
F - 20.	CLEAVE	T.	To punish
V - 21.	HARBINGER	U.	Easily perceived
Y - 22.	COURIERS	V.	One that indicates what is to come
P - 23.	PURGED	W.	Evil; wicked
C - 24.	EQUIVOCATES	X.	Immoderate desire for wealth
G - 25.	INTERDICTION	Y.	A messenger

Copyrighted

Macbeth Vocabulary Matching 4

___ 1. AGUE A. To free from impurities
___ 2. CAROUSING B. Easily perceived
___ 3. MUSE C. A messenger
___ 4. SUBORNED D. Drunken merrymaking
___ 5. BRANDISHED E. To consider
___ 6. INTEGRITY F. To hesitate as a result of conscience
___ 7. BEGUILE G. To punish
___ 8. EQUIVOCATES H. Induced to commit an unlawful act
___ 9. CORPORAL I. Steadfast adherence to a strict moral code
___ 10. MINION J. To fill with dismay
___ 11. CALDRON K. Extremely small in size
___ 12. SCRUPLES L. To adhere, cling or stick fast
___ 13. PALPABLE M. The murdering of one's father, mother or relative
___ 14. PERNICIOUS N. Evil; wicked
___ 15. DIMINUTIVE O. To wave or flourish
___ 16. MALICE P. A large vessel
___ 17. PARRICIDE Q. To pass (time) pleasantly
___ 18. HOMAGE R. A chill or fit of shivering
___ 19. CHASTISE S. An obsequious follower
___ 20. COURIERS T. One that indicates what is to come
___ 21. CENSURES U. Of or relating to the body
___ 22. HARBINGER V. Special honor expressed publicly
___ 23. CLEAVE W. Extreme ill will or spite
___ 24. PURGED X. To avoid making an explicit statement
___ 25. APPALL Y. Harsh criticisms

Macbeth Vocabulary Matching 4 Answer Key

R - 1.	AGUE	A.	To free from impurities
D - 2.	CAROUSING	B.	Easily perceived
E - 3.	MUSE	C.	A messenger
H - 4.	SUBORNED	D.	Drunken merrymaking
O - 5.	BRANDISHED	E.	To consider
I - 6.	INTEGRITY	F.	To hesitate as a result of conscience
Q - 7.	BEGUILE	G.	To punish
X - 8.	EQUIVOCATES	H.	Induced to commit an unlawful act
U - 9.	CORPORAL	I.	Steadfast adherence to a strict moral code
S - 10.	MINION	J.	To fill with dismay
P - 11.	CALDRON	K.	Extremely small in size
F - 12.	SCRUPLES	L.	To adhere, cling or stick fast
B - 13.	PALPABLE	M.	The murdering of one's father, mother or relative
N - 14.	PERNICIOUS	N.	Evil; wicked
K - 15.	DIMINUTIVE	O.	To wave or flourish
W - 16.	MALICE	P.	A large vessel
M - 17.	PARRICIDE	Q.	To pass (time) pleasantly
V - 18.	HOMAGE	R.	A chill or fit of shivering
G - 19.	CHASTISE	S.	An obsequious follower
C - 20.	COURIERS	T.	One that indicates what is to come
Y - 21.	CENSURES	U.	Of or relating to the body
T - 22.	HARBINGER	V.	Special honor expressed publicly
L - 23.	CLEAVE	W.	Extreme ill will or spite
A - 24.	PURGED	X.	To avoid making an explicit statement
J - 25.	APPALL	Y.	Harsh criticisms

Macbeth Vocabulary Magic Squares 1

Match the definition with the vocabulary word. Put your answers in the magic squares below. When your answers are correct, all columns and rows will add to the same number.

A. COURIERS
B. INTEGRITY
C. MUSE
D. AGUE
E. CAROUSING
F. AVARICIOUS
G. APPEASE
H. MALICE
I. HARBINGER
J. CHASTISE
K. APPALL
L. PALPABLE
M. SUBORNED
N. MINION
O. BIDES
P. CALDRON

1. To wait
2. To punish
3. Extreme ill will or spite
4. A messenger
5. A chill or fit of shivering
6. Drunken merrymaking
7. To fill with dismay
8. An obsequious follower
9. Immoderate desire for wealth
10. To consider
11. Induced to commit an unlawful act
12. Easily perceived
13. One that indicates what is to come
14. A large vessel
15. Steadfast adherence to a strict moral code
16. To bring peace

A=	B=	C=	D=
E=	F=	G=	H=
I=	J=	K=	L=
M=	N=	O=	P=

78
Copyrighted

Macbeth Vocabulary Magic Squares 1 Answer Key

Match the definition with the vocabulary word. Put your answers in the magic squares below. When your answers are correct, all columns and rows will add to the same number.

A. COURIERS
B. INTEGRITY
C. MUSE
D. AGUE
E. CAROUSING
F. AVARICIOUS
G. APPEASE
H. MALICE
I. HARBINGER
J. CHASTISE
K. APPALL
L. PALPABLE
M. SUBORNED
N. MINION
O. BIDES
P. CALDRON

1. To wait
2. To punish
3. Extreme ill will or spite
4. A messenger
5. A chill or fit of shivering
6. Drunken merrymaking
7. To fill with dismay
8. An obsequious follower
9. Immoderate desire for wealth
10. To consider
11. Induced to commit an unlawful act
12. Easily perceived
13. One that indicates what is to come
14. A large vessel
15. Steadfast adherence to a strict moral code
16. To bring peace

A=4	B=15	C=10	D=5
E=6	F=9	G=16	H=3
I=13	J=2	K=7	L=12
M=11	N=8	O=1	P=14

Macbeth Vocabulary Magic Squares 2

Match the definition with the vocabulary word. Put your answers in the magic squares below. When your answers are correct, all columns and rows will add to the same number.

A. AGUE
B. PERNICIOUS
C. MALICE
D. CORPORAL
E. INTEGRITY
F. VIZARDS
G. CLEAVE
H. COURIERS
I. DEFTLY
J. MUSE
K. APPEASE
L. PURGED
M. MINION
N. EQUIVOCATES
O. APPALL
P. BRANDISHED

1. An obsequious follower
2. Mask
3. A messenger
4. To fill with dismay
5. To free from impurities
6. Extreme ill will or spite
7. A chill or fit of shivering
8. To consider
9. To bring peace
10. Of or relating to the body
11. Evil; wicked
12. Quickly and skillfully
13. To avoid making an explicit statement
14. Steadfast adherence to a strict moral code
15. To adhere, cling or stick fast
16. To wave or flourish

A=	B=	C=	D=
E=	F=	G=	H=
I=	J=	K=	L=
M=	N=	O=	P=

80
Copyrighted

Macbeth Vocabulary Magic Squares 2 Answer Key

Match the definition with the vocabulary word. Put your answers in the magic squares below. When your answers are correct, all columns and rows will add to the same number.

A. AGUE
B. PERNICIOUS
C. MALICE
D. CORPORAL
E. INTEGRITY
F. VIZARDS
G. CLEAVE
H. COURIERS
I. DEFTLY
J. MUSE
K. APPEASE
L. PURGED
M. MINION
N. EQUIVOCATES
O. APPALL
P. BRANDISHED

1. An obsequious follower
2. Mask
3. A messenger
4. To fill with dismay
5. To free from impurities
6. Extreme ill will or spite
7. A chill or fit of shivering
8. To consider
9. To bring peace
10. Of or relating to the body
11. Evil; wicked
12. Quickly and skillfully
13. To avoid making an explicit statement
14. Steadfast adherence to a strict moral code
15. To adhere, cling or stick fast
16. To wave or flourish

A=7	B=11	C=6	D=10
E=14	F=2	G=15	H=3
I=12	J=8	K=9	L=5
M=1	N=13	O=4	P=16

Macbeth Vocabulary Magic Squares 3

Match the definition with the vocabulary word. Put your answers in the magic squares below. When your answers are correct, all columns and rows will add to the same number.

A. MALICE   E. HOMAGE   I. VIZARDS   M. MINION
B. CENSURES   F. INTERDICTION   J. HARBINGER   N. SCRUPLES
C. CHASTISE   G. CALDRON   K. DEFTLY   O. APPALL
D. EQUIVOCATES   H. BRANDISHED   L. INTEGRITY   P. APPEASE

1. To wave or flourish
2. An obsequious follower
3. Harsh criticisms
4. Quickly and skillfully
5. One that indicates what is to come
6. To punish
7. To bring peace
8. Special honor expressed publicly
9. To fill with dismay
10. To forbid authoritatively
11. Mask
12. To avoid making an explicit statement
13. Extreme ill will or spite
14. Steadfast adherence to a strict moral code
15. A large vessel
16. To hesitate as a result of conscience

A=	B=	C=	D=
E=	F=	G=	H=
I=	J=	K=	L=
M=	N=	O=	P=

Macbeth Vocabulary Magic Squares 3 Answer Key

Match the definition with the vocabulary word. Put your answers in the magic squares below. When your answers are correct, all columns and rows will add to the same number.

A. MALICE
B. CENSURES
C. CHASTISE
D. EQUIVOCATES
E. HOMAGE
F. INTERDICTION
G. CALDRON
H. BRANDISHED
I. VIZARDS
J. HARBINGER
K. DEFTLY
L. INTEGRITY
M. MINION
N. SCRUPLES
O. APPALL
P. APPEASE

1. To wave or flourish
2. An obsequious follower
3. Harsh criticisms
4. Quickly and skillfully
5. One that indicates what is to come
6. To punish
7. To bring peace
8. Special honor expressed publicly
9. To fill with dismay
10. To forbid authoritatively
11. Mask
12. To avoid making an explicit statement
13. Extreme ill will or spite
14. Steadfast adherence to a strict moral code
15. A large vessel
16. To hesitate as a result of conscience

A=13	B=3	C=6	D=12
E=8	F=10	G=15	H=1
I=11	J=5	K=4	L=14
M=2	N=16	O=9	P=7

Macbeth Vocabulary Magic Squares 4

Match the definition with the vocabulary word. Put your answers in the magic squares below. When your answers are correct, all columns and rows will add to the same number.

A. VIZARDS   E. SCRUPLES   I. SUBORNED   M. CLEAVE
B. HARBINGER F. APPEASE   J. DIMINUTIVE   N. MUSE
C. DEFTLY   G. AVARICIOUS   K. EQUIVOCATES   O. AGUE
D. PALPABLE   H. PARRICIDE   L. CHASTISE   P. MALICE

1. The murdering of one's father, mother or relative
2. Mask
3. One that indicates what is to come
4. Immoderate desire for wealth
5. Extremely small in size
6. A chill or fit of shivering
7. Extreme ill will or spite
8. Induced to commit an unlawful act
9. To avoid making an explicit statement
10. To consider
11. To adhere, cling or stick fast
12. To punish
13. To hesitate as a result of conscience
14. Easily perceived
15. Quickly and skillfully
16. To bring peace

A=	B=	C=	D=
E=	F=	G=	H=
I=	J=	K=	L=
M=	N=	O=	P=

Macbeth Vocabulary Magic Squares 4 Answer Key

Match the definition with the vocabulary word. Put your answers in the magic squares below. When your answers are correct, all columns and rows will add to the same number.

A. VIZARDS   E. SCRUPLES   I. SUBORNED   M. CLEAVE
B. HARBINGER   F. APPEASE   J. DIMINUTIVE   N. MUSE
C. DEFTLY   G. AVARICIOUS   K. EQUIVOCATES   O. AGUE
D. PALPABLE   H. PARRICIDE   L. CHASTISE   P. MALICE

1. The murdering of one's father, mother or relative
2. Mask
3. One that indicates what is to come
4. Immoderate desire for wealth
5. Extremely small in size
6. A chill or fit of shivering
7. Extreme ill will or spite
8. Induced to commit an unlawful act
9. To avoid making an explicit statement
10. To consider
11. To adhere, cling or stick fast
12. To punish
13. To hesitate as a result of conscience
14. Easily perceived
15. Quickly and skillfully
16. To bring peace

A=2	B=3	C=15	D=14
E=13	F=16	G=4	H=1
I=8	J=5	K=9	L=12
M=11	N=10	O=6	P=7

Macbeth Vocabulary Word Search 1

Words are placed backwards, forward, diagonally, up and down. Clues listed below can help you find the words. Circle the hidden vocabulary words in the maze.

```
V L R P M N L I J G F H G N N J R N K F
W G L Z Z T V S N C X N F W Y G C H G P
K K C Z S P J R W T I X F C L G H H F J
R L X N E C C D V S E P S L Z T G R B X
M D Y T L V P L U B K G U H T H K P C X
H A E N P S X O E A K K R J X Q A O N
S D L J U N R Q H A P Y C I G P H L R Y
D I I I R A W K P N V P H G T E G P P D
E M U Z C A L D R O N E A Q S Y D A O H
H I G L S E R Z C G D S L H A H B R J
S N E G D E P Z E A M I T F L G A L A X
I U B H D M S N M I Q C I D A U R E L V
D T B I Q D S O N K G I S Q P E B I P Y
N I B O R U H I K J F R E L P D I N E H
A V T A R W O M U S E R C V E E N T R X
R E Z E R N Y J U N Q A O Q A F G E N S
B I S P T Y E O D Q T P U Q S T E R I Y
V T F D P B I D N D B I R G E L R D C D
S J J L T C R Q N K V D I R G Y G I I W
T S N S I J Z C M O N Q E Z P C W C O X
T C M R T Z C L C Z J Z R W Q T M T U L
P P A R D C J A D V C C S K S K M I S S
V V B V Z N T H Y L T M D D S G V O Z W
A H N Y R E K T X M M J N Q T B F N S R
Y M Z M S J W C P M T W B J C Y Q G P R
```

A chill or fit of shivering (4)
A large vessel (7)
A messenger (8)
An obsequious follower (6)
Drunken merrymaking (9)
Easily perceived (8)
Evil; wicked (10)
Extreme ill will or spite (6)
Extremely small in size (10)
Harsh criticisms (8)
Immoderate desire for wealth (10)
Induced to commit an unlawful act (8)
Mask (7)
Of or relating to the body (8)
One that indicates what is to come (9)
Quickly and skillfully (6)
Special honor expressed publicly (6)
Steadfast adherence to a strict moral code (9)
The murdering of one's father, mother or relative (9)

To adhere, cling or stick fast (6)
To avoid making an explicit statement (11)
To bring peace (7)
To consider (4)
To fill with dismay (6)
To forbid authoritatively (12)
To free from impurities (6)
To hesitate as a result of conscience (8)
To pass (time) pleasantly (7)
To punish (8)
To wait (5)
To wave or flourish (10)

Macbeth Vocabulary Word Search 1 Answer Key

Words are placed backwards, forward, diagonally, up and down. Clues listed below can help you find the words. Circle the hidden vocabulary words in the maze.

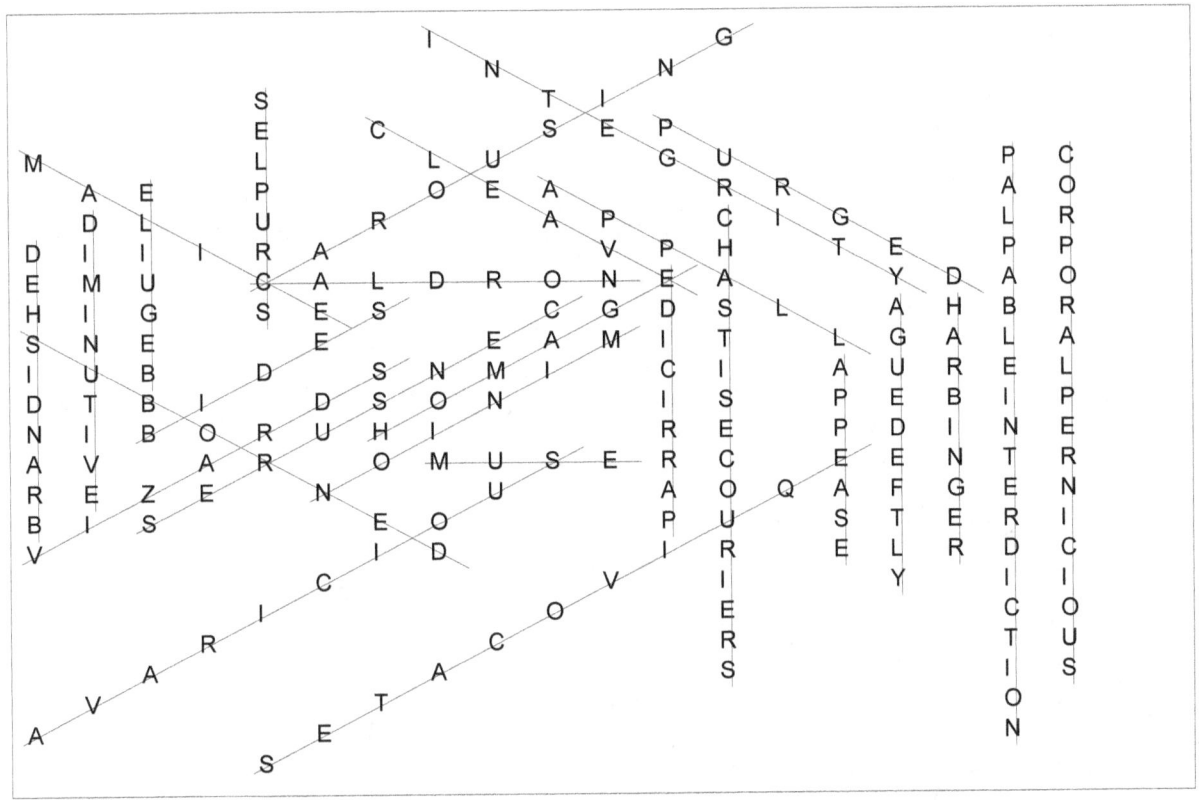

A chill or fit of shivering (4)
A large vessel (7)
A messenger (8)
An obsequious follower (6)
Drunken merrymaking (9)
Easily perceived (8)
Evil; wicked (10)
Extreme ill will or spite (6)
Extremely small in size (10)
Harsh criticisms (8)
Immoderate desire for wealth (10)
Induced to commit an unlawful act (8)
Mask (7)
Of or relating to the body (8)
One that indicates what is to come (9)
Quickly and skillfully (6)
Special honor expressed publicly (6)
Steadfast adherence to a strict moral code (9)
The murdering of one's father, mother or relative (9)

To adhere, cling or stick fast (6)
To avoid making an explicit statement (11)
To bring peace (7)
To consider (4)
To fill with dismay (6)
To forbid authoritatively (12)
To free from impurities (6)
To hesitate as a result of conscience (8)
To pass (time) pleasantly (7)
To punish (8)
To wait (5)
To wave or flourish (10)

Macbeth Vocabulary Crossword 2

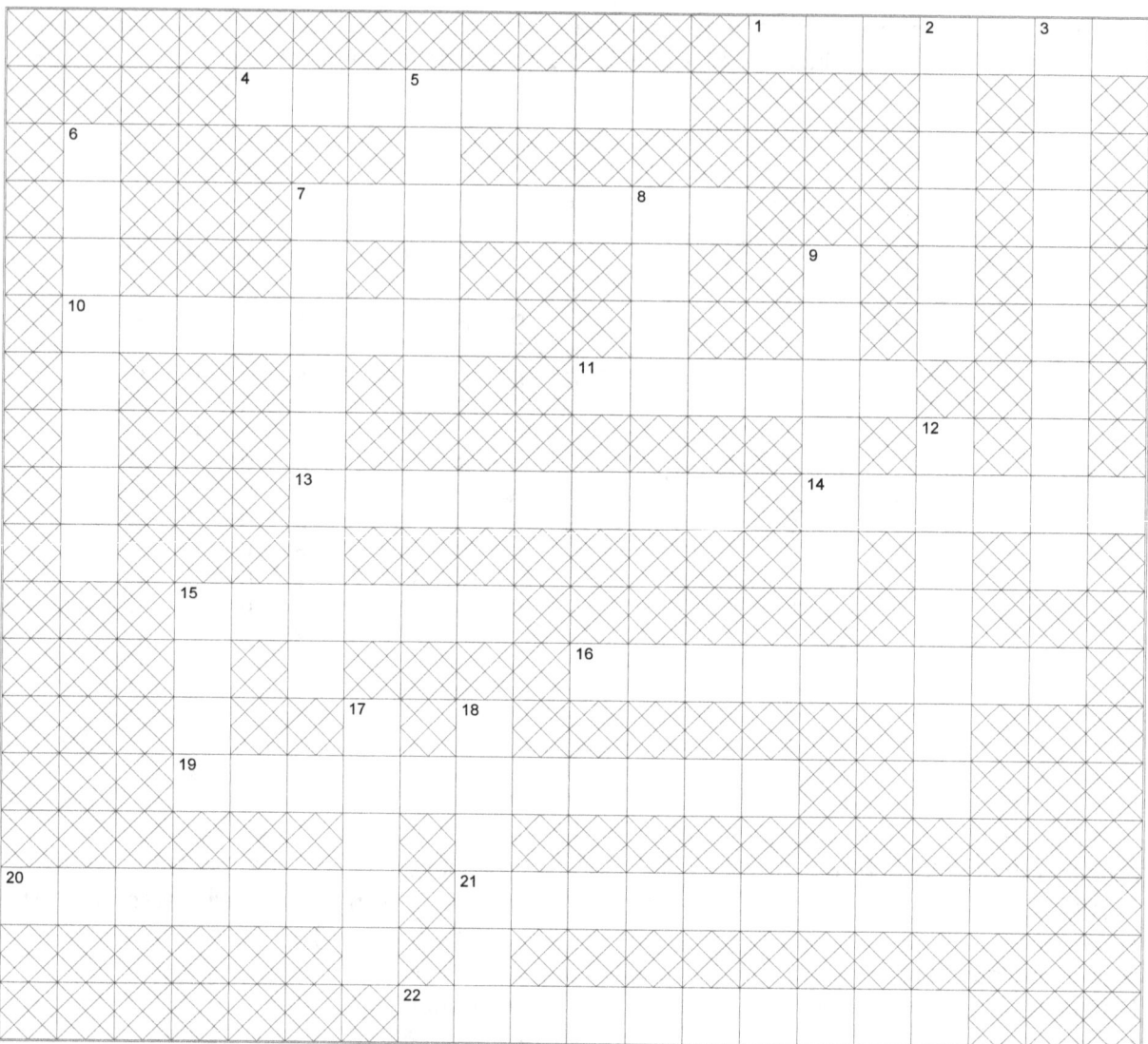

Across
1. Mask
4. Easily perceived
7. Of or relating to the body
10. Induced to commit an unlawful act
11. Quickly and skillfully
13. To hesitate as a result of conscience
14. To adhere, cling or stick fast
15. An obsequious follower
16. The murdering of one's father, mother or relative
19. To avoid making an explicit statement
20. To bring peace
21. Immoderate desire for wealth
22. Evil; wicked

Down
2. To fill with dismay
3. Extremely small in size
5. To free from impurities
6. Harsh criticisms
7. Drunken merrymaking
8. A chill or fit of shivering
9. Extreme ill will or spite
12. To pass (time) pleasantly
15. To consider
17. To wait
18. Special honor expressed publicly

Macbeth Vocabulary Crossword 2 Answer Key

									1 V	I	2 A	R	3 D	S
			4 P	A	L	5 P	A	B	L	E			P			I	
6 C						U						P		M
E			7 C	O	R	P	O	R	8 A	L		A		I
N				A		G			G		9 M		L		N
10 S	U	B	O	R	N	E	D		U		A		L		U
U				O		D		11 D	E	F	T	L	Y		T
R				U							I		12 B		I
E			13 S	C	R	U	P	L	E	S		14 C	L	E	A	V	E
S				I							E		G		E
		15 M	I	N	I	O	N						U		
		U		G			16 P	A	R	R	I	C	I	D	E
		S		17 B		18 H						L		
		19 E	Q	U	I	V	O	C	A	T	E	S			E		
				D		M								
20 A	P	P	E	A	S	E		21 A	V	A	R	I	C	I	O	U	S
				S		G								
				22 P	E	R	N	I	C	I	O	U	S	

Across
1. Mask
4. Easily perceived
7. Of or relating to the body
10. Induced to commit an unlawful act
11. Quickly and skillfully
13. To hesitate as a result of conscience
14. To adhere, cling or stick fast
15. An obsequious follower
16. The murdering of one's father, mother or relative
19. To avoid making an explicit statement
20. To bring peace
21. Immoderate desire for wealth
22. Evil; wicked

Down
2. To fill with dismay
3. Extremely small in size
5. To free from impurities
6. Harsh criticisms
7. Drunken merrymaking
8. A chill or fit of shivering
9. Extreme ill will or spite
12. To pass (time) pleasantly
15. To consider
17. To wait
18. Special honor expressed publicly

Macbeth Vocabulary Word Search 3

Words are placed backwards, forward, diagonally, up and down. Words listed below are included in the maze. Circle the hidden vocabulary words in the maze.

```
I N T E G R I T Y M C H D D A P A E B J
T G Z W A D V J B Q O A I E P A P Q T T
F Q S B V J T Q Y M U R M F P L P U F G
Z G S M A C V L A U R B I T A P E I F X
C F K V R T F G G S I I N L L A A V N K
Q R P T I S E S P E E N U Y L B S O K V
N X X J C H P N L P R G T S R L E C G Y
C F D H I R T N C S S E I R W E W A D T
F V V N O R D L A C W R V J M H Q T B R
C P K G U T S G G F M Y E V F M X E K S
B Y N V S L J L G C Y S K C X T K S R C
R J H Y J G H P G L G D N V S Z R F S E
K M Z P V Q M Q M N K E P M U H S F W N
P H R K S M N I I E G H J A O C L S Q S
L H Z L K B B S N D K S K L I Z L E S U
T F C H K Z U N N I D I K I C G D D M R
M H Y O D O K G T C O D F C I M V I T E
I N T E R D I C T I O N D E N R O B U S
Z Z R A B P L X L R B A N J R B C B E E
S C C Y K P O Y N F R L K E E K L U E E
R F J C L B W R Y A P B Q C P G P G V M
C H A S T I S E A P U R G E D U A A X K
Q V Q F Z X Y H X L B P F W R I E M G P
K Y B W C M H C P S K M G C S L M V V W
V I Z A R D S G G L B C S X C E N K Q V
```

AGUE	CAROUSING	EQUIVOCATES	PALPABLE
APPALL	CENSURES	HARBINGER	PARRICIDE
APPEASE	CHASTISE	HOMAGE	PERNICIOUS
AVARICIOUS	CLEAVE	INTEGRITY	PURGED
BEGUILE	CORPORAL	INTERDICTION	SCRUPLES
BIDES	COURIERS	MALICE	SUBORNED
BRANDISHED	DEFTLY	MINION	VIZARDS
CALDRON	DIMINUTIVE	MUSE	

Macbeth Vocabulary Word Search 3 Answer Key

Words are placed backwards, forward, diagonally, up and down. Words listed below are included in the maze. Circle the hidden vocabulary words in the maze.

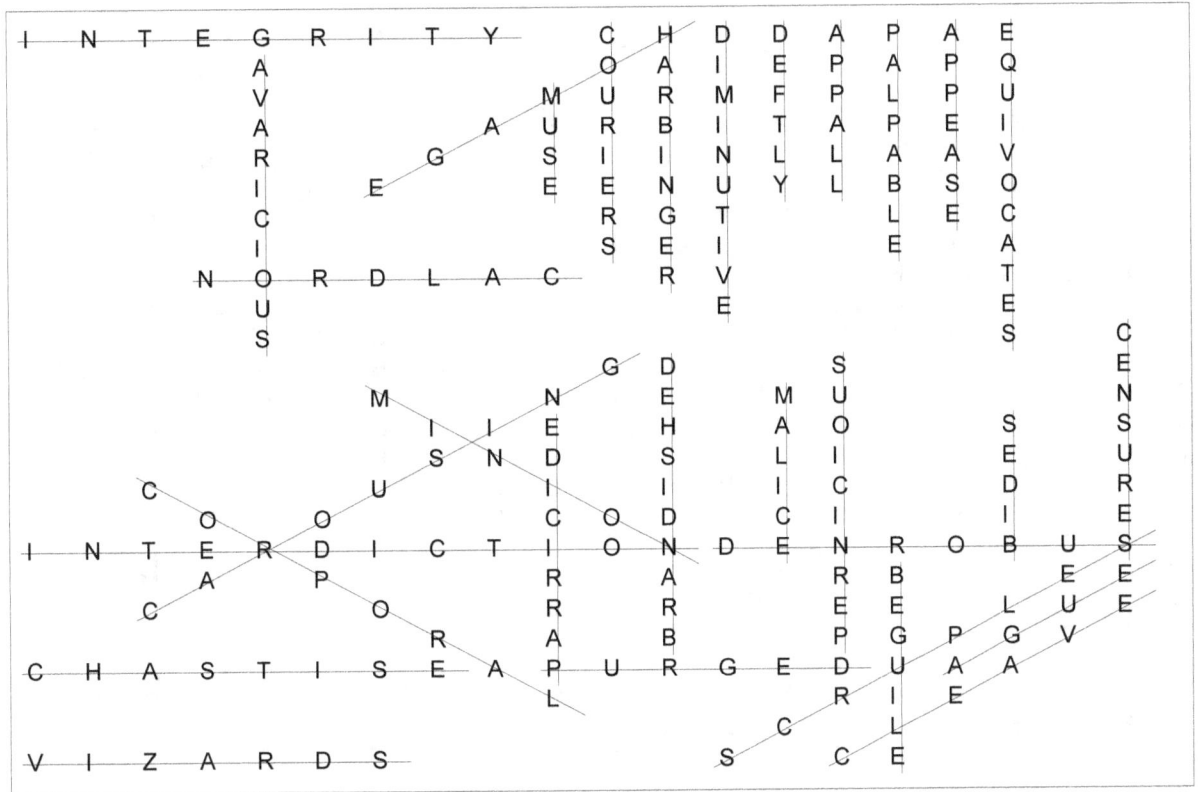

AGUE	CAROUSING	EQUIVOCATES	PALPABLE
APPALL	CENSURES	HARBINGER	PARRICIDE
APPEASE	CHASTISE	HOMAGE	PERNICIOUS
AVARICIOUS	CLEAVE	INTEGRITY	PURGED
BEGUILE	CORPORAL	INTERDICTION	SCRUPLES
BIDES	COURIERS	MALICE	SUBORNED
BRANDISHED	DEFTLY	MINION	VIZARDS
CALDRON	DIMINUTIVE	MUSE	

Macbeth Vocabulary Word Search 4

Words are placed backwards, forward, diagonally, up and down. Words listed below are included in the maze. Circle the hidden vocabulary words in the maze.

```
P M F R W N C O R P O R A L N S B B G P
S E K J Q V D K B C P B J V M N N B B S
C W R J K V C F M F L T H C C D T N P R
L F J N J X N P K M F R R P Q C P B F M
N N K T I E Q U I V O C A T E S L L T D
Q B R M B C F Z D Q B R D K F W M S K J
G S C H Z V I B P G J R M W G T B W G Q
B U P O J B J O T V M E W C B P H N S F
V B D H U F W I U T T G V L T C I Z S T
N O Y O Q R L N S S Z N F W A S Z D M J
I R R M A K I T A R S I V L U B F T E G
K N C A C V K E K P W B D O H L B J C L
Q E T G S H A G R X P R R B D E R M I Q
K D C E N S U R E S O A G U E V A E L C
V G D S R P R I I N C H L L F I N S A Q
M I P J Y D V T P C D G B L T T D I M C
B M U S E A I Y S Q I A D W L U I T L B
P F R B D P Z C H C P O N Z Y N S S C H
W N G E I P A Y T L R D U S K I H A M H
M M E G C E R D A I N U R S G M E H F V
T Q D U I A D P X S O G P N T I D C X X
C S Z I R S S F L T I N F L S D P N Z F
P Y Z L R E T X H J N V X K E W R R S F
X X H E A D L Z W R I R L F J S Z T Q V
Z V F F P N F S Y L M J D M C K G V Y Q
```

AGUE   CAROUSING   EQUIVOCATES   PALPABLE

APPALL   CENSURES   HARBINGER   PARRICIDE

APPEASE   CHASTISE   HOMAGE   PERNICIOUS

AVARICIOUS   CLEAVE   INTEGRITY   PURGED

BEGUILE   CORPORAL   INTERDICTION   SCRUPLES

BIDES   COURIERS   MALICE   SUBORNED

BRANDISHED   DEFTLY   MINION   VIZARDS

CALDRON   DIMINUTIVE   MUSE

Copyrighted

Macbeth Vocabulary Word Search 4 Answer Key

Words are placed backwards, forward, diagonally, up and down. Words listed below are included in the maze. Circle the hidden vocabulary words in the maze.

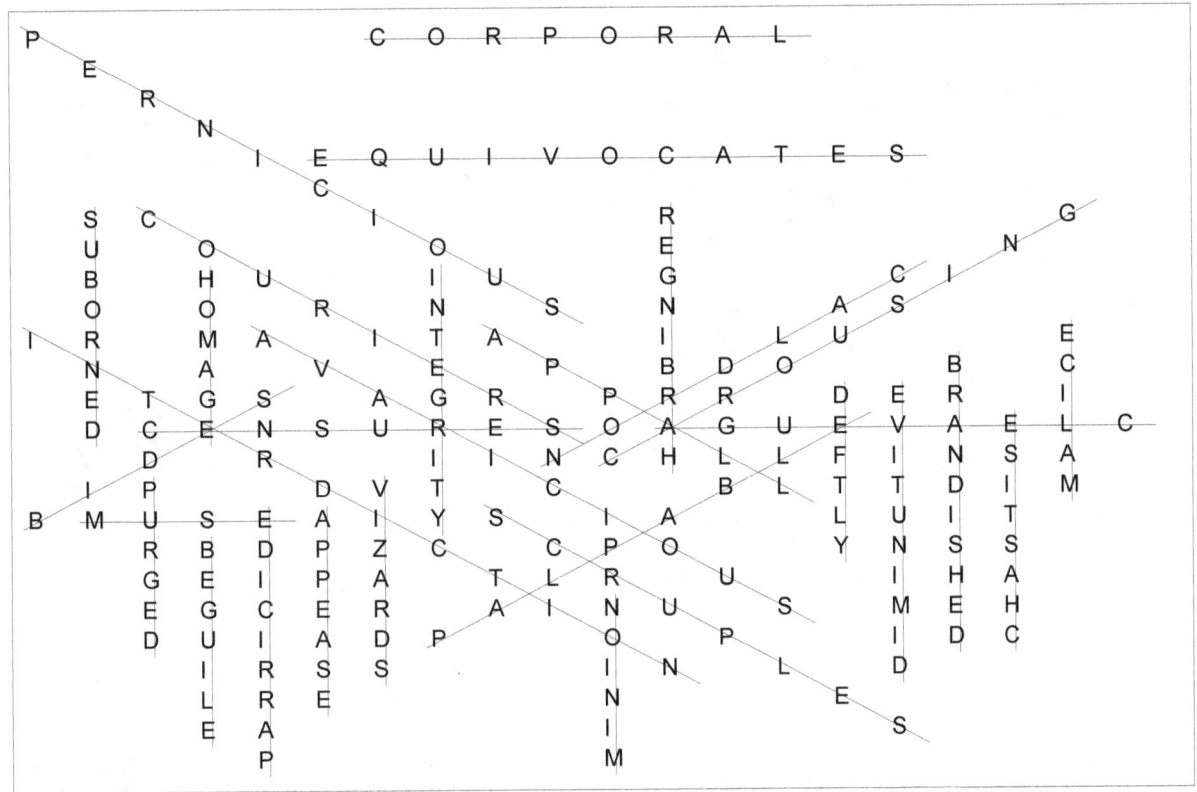

AGUE	CAROUSING	EQUIVOCATES	PALPABLE
APPALL	CENSURES	HARBINGER	PARRICIDE
APPEASE	CHASTISE	HOMAGE	PERNICIOUS
AVARICIOUS	CLEAVE	INTEGRITY	PURGED
BEGUILE	CORPORAL	INTERDICTION	SCRUPLES
BIDES	COURIERS	MALICE	SUBORNED
BRANDISHED	DEFTLY	MINION	VIZARDS
CALDRON	DIMINUTIVE	MUSE	

Macbeth Vocabulary Crossword 1

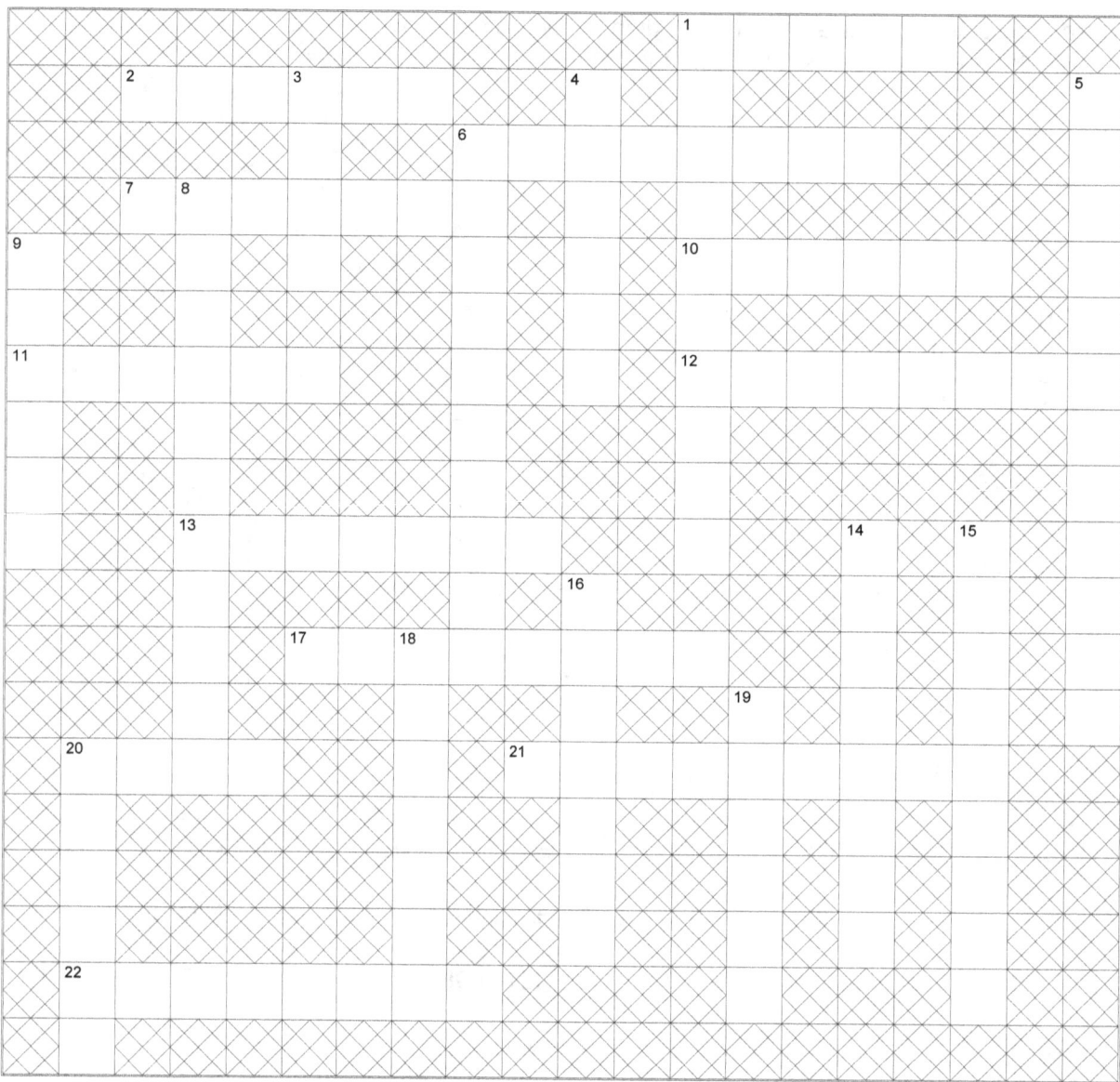

Across
1. To wait
2. To fill with dismay
6. Easily perceived
7. To pass (time) pleasantly
10. Quickly and skillfully
11. An obsequious follower
12. Induced to commit an unlawful act
13. A large vessel
17. To punish
20. To consider
21. Drunken merrymaking
22. Harsh criticisms

Down
1. To wave or flourish
3. A chill or fit of shivering
4. To adhere, cling or stick fast
5. To forbid authoritatively
6. Evil; wicked
8. To avoid making an explicit statement
9. Special honor expressed publicly
14. A messenger
15. Steadfast adherence to a strict moral code
16. Mask
18. To bring peace
19. To free from impurities
20. Extreme ill will or spite

Macbeth Vocabulary Crossword 1 Answer Key

(Crossword grid with answers filled in:)

- 1 Across: BIDES
- 2 Across: APPALL
- 6 Across: PALPABLE
- 7 Across: BEGUILE
- 10 Across: DEFTLY
- 11 Across: MINION
- 12 Across: SUBORNED
- 13 Across: CALDRON
- 17 Across: CHASTISE
- 20 Across: MUSE
- 21 Across: CAROUSING
- 22 Across: CENSURES

- 1 Down: BRANDISH
- 3 Down: AGUE
- 4 Down: CLEAVE
- 5 Down: INTERDICT
- 6 Down: PERNICIOUS
- 8 Down: EQUIVOCATE
- 9 Down: HOMAGE
- 14 Down: COURIER
- 15 Down: INTEGRITY
- 16 Down: VIZED (VIZER)
- 18 Down: APPEASE
- 19 Down: PURGE
- 20 Down: MALICE

Across
1. To wait
2. To fill with dismay
6. Easily perceived
7. To pass (time) pleasantly
10. Quickly and skillfully
11. An obsequious follower
12. Induced to commit an unlawful act
13. A large vessel
17. To punish
20. To consider
21. Drunken merrymaking
22. Harsh criticisms

Down
1. To wave or flourish
3. A chill or fit of shivering
4. To adhere, cling or stick fast
5. To forbid authoritatively
6. Evil; wicked
8. To avoid making an explicit statement
9. Special honor expressed publicly
14. A messenger
15. Steadfast adherence to a strict moral code
16. Mask
18. To bring peace
19. To free from impurities
20. Extreme ill will or spite

Macbeth Vocabulary Crossword 2

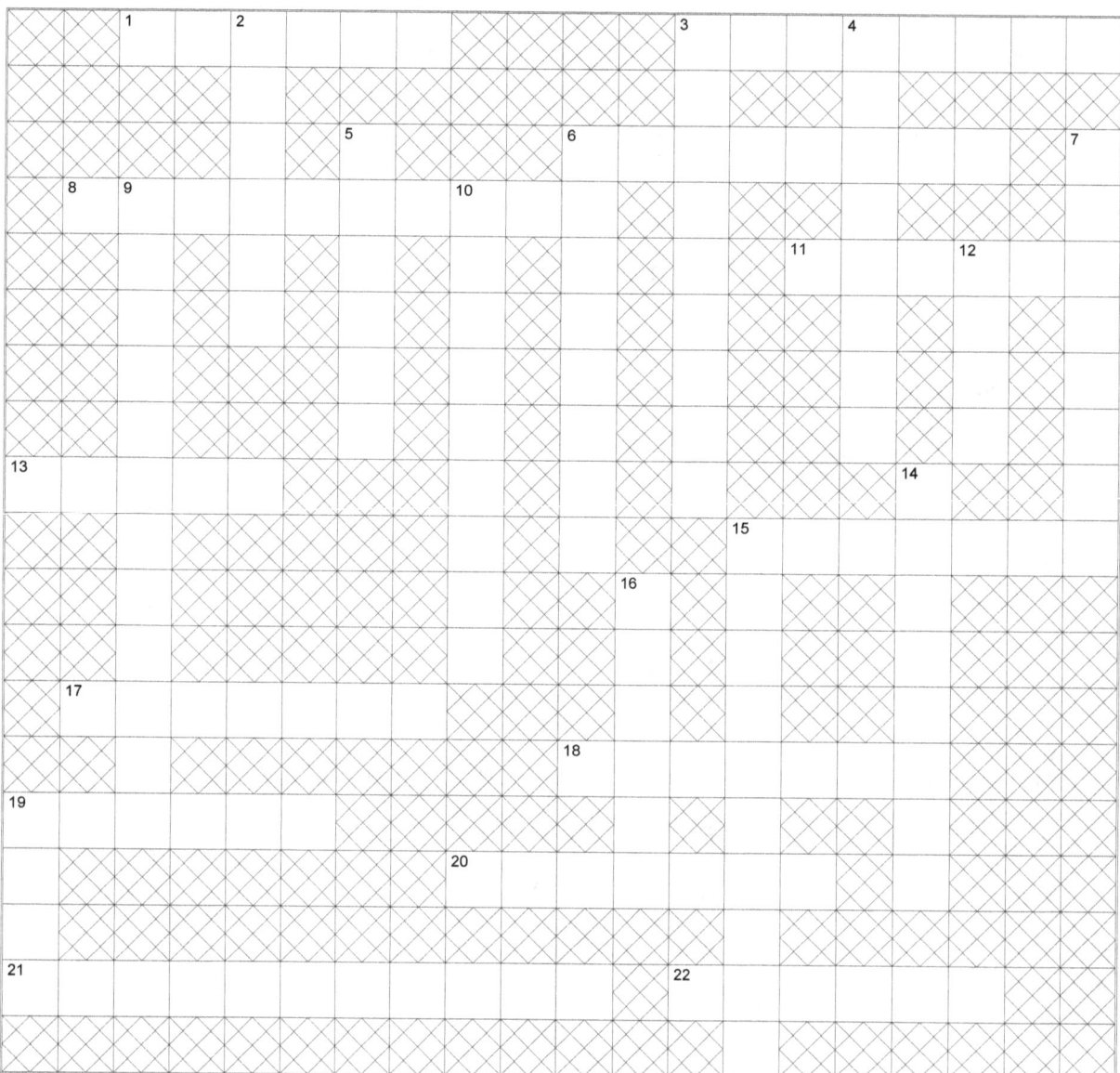

Across
1. Special honor expressed publicly
3. To punish
6. Of or relating to the body
8. Extremely small in size
11. To fill with dismay
13. To wait
15. To pass (time) pleasantly
17. Mask
18. A large vessel
19. An obsequious follower
20. To bring peace
21. To avoid making an explicit statement
22. Quickly and skillfully

Down
2. Extreme ill will or spite
3. Drunken merrymaking
4. To hesitate as a result of conscience
5. To free from impurities
6. Harsh criticisms
7. Easily perceived
9. To forbid authoritatively
10. Steadfast adherence to a strict moral code
12. A chill or fit of shivering
14. Induced to commit an unlawful act
15. To wave or flourish
16. To adhere, cling or stick fast
19. To consider

Macbeth Vocabulary Crossword 2 Answer Key

	1 H	2 O	M	A	G	E			3 C	H	A	4 S	T	I	S	E
			A						A			C				
			L	5 P		6 C	O	R	P	O	R	A	L			7 P
8 D	9 I	M	I	N	U	T	I	V	E			U		11 A	12 P	A
	N		C	R		N			N			L		P	P	L
	T		E	G		T			S			E		P	A	L
	E			E		E			U			S		L	L	P
	R			D		G			R					E	U	A
13 B	I	D	E	S		R			E				14 S		E	B
	I					I			S		15 B	E	G	U	I	L	E
	C					T				16 C		R			B	
	T					Y				L		A			O	
17 V	I	Z	A	R	D	S				E		N			R	
	O							18 C	A	L	D	R	O	N	
19 M	I	N	I	O	N			V		I				E	
U					20 A	P	P	E	A	S	E		D		
S										H					
21 E	Q	U	I	V	O	C	A	T	E	S		22 D	E	F	T	L	Y
												D				

Across
1. Special honor expressed publicly
3. To punish
6. Of or relating to the body
8. Extremely small in size
11. To fill with dismay
13. To wait
15. To pass (time) pleasantly
17. Mask
18. A large vessel
19. An obsequious follower
20. To bring peace
21. To avoid making an explicit statement
22. Quickly and skillfully

Down
2. Extreme ill will or spite
3. Drunken merrymaking
4. To hesitate as a result of conscience
5. To free from impurities
6. Harsh criticisms
7. Easily perceived
9. To forbid authoritatively
10. Steadfast adherence to a strict moral code
12. A chill or fit of shivering
14. Induced to commit an unlawful act
15. To wave or flourish
16. To adhere, cling or stick fast
19. To consider

Macbeth Vocabulary Crossword 3

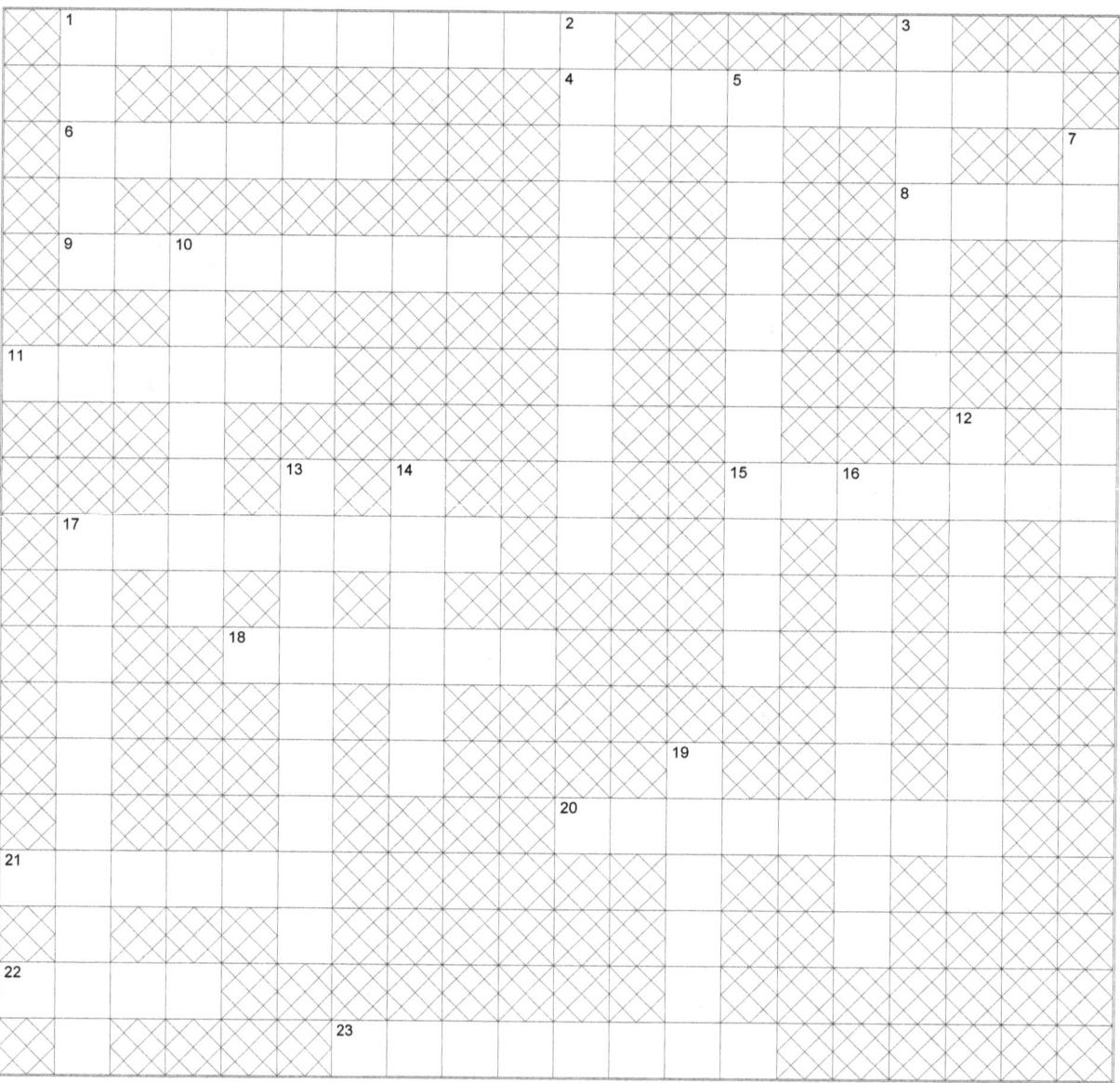

Across
1. To wave or flourish
4. Steadfast adherence to a strict moral code
6. Quickly and skillfully
8. A chill or fit of shivering
9. Induced to commit an unlawful act
11. To free from impurities
15. To bring peace
17. Easily perceived
18. Special honor expressed publicly
20. To punish
21. An obsequious follower
22. To consider
23. To hesitate as a result of conscience

Down
1. To wait
2. Extremely small in size
3. Mask
5. To avoid making an explicit statement
7. Harsh criticisms
10. To pass (time) pleasantly
12. One that indicates what is to come
13. Drunken merrymaking
14. To adhere, cling or stick fast
16. The murdering of one's father, mother or relative
17. Evil; wicked
19. Extreme ill will or spite

Macbeth Vocabulary Crossword 3 Answer Key

	1 B	R	A	N	D	I	S	H	E	2 D			3 V		
	I								4 I	N	T	5 E	G	R	I	T	Y
	6 D	E	F	T	L	Y			M			Q			Z		7 C
	E								I			U			8 A	G	U	E
	9 S	U	10 B	O	R	N	E	D		N			I			R		N
			E							U			V			D		S
11 P	U	R	G	E	D					T			O			S		U
			U							I			C			12 H		R
			I		13 C		14 C			V			15 A	P	16 P	E	A	S	E
	17 P	A	L	P	A	B	L	E			E			T		A		R		S
	E				E		R		E					E		R		B		
	R				18 H	O	M	A	G	E				S		R		I		
	N						U		V							I		N		
	I						S		E					19 M		C		G		
	C						I					20 C	H	A	S	T	I	S	E
21 M	I	N	I	O	N									L		D		R		
	O						G							I		E				
22 M	U	S	E											C						
	S			23 S	C	R	U	P	L	E	S									

Across
1. To wave or flourish
4. Steadfast adherence to a strict moral code
6. Quickly and skillfully
8. A chill or fit of shivering
9. Induced to commit an unlawful act
11. To free from impurities
15. To bring peace
17. Easily perceived
18. Special honor expressed publicly
20. To punish
21. An obsequious follower
22. To consider
23. To hesitate as a result of conscience

Down
1. To wait
2. Extremely small in size
3. Mask
5. To avoid making an explicit statement
7. Harsh criticisms
10. To pass (time) pleasantly
12. One that indicates what is to come
13. Drunken merrymaking
14. To adhere, cling or stick fast
16. The murdering of one's father, mother or relative
17. Evil; wicked
19. Extreme ill will or spite

Macbeth Vocabulary Crossword 4

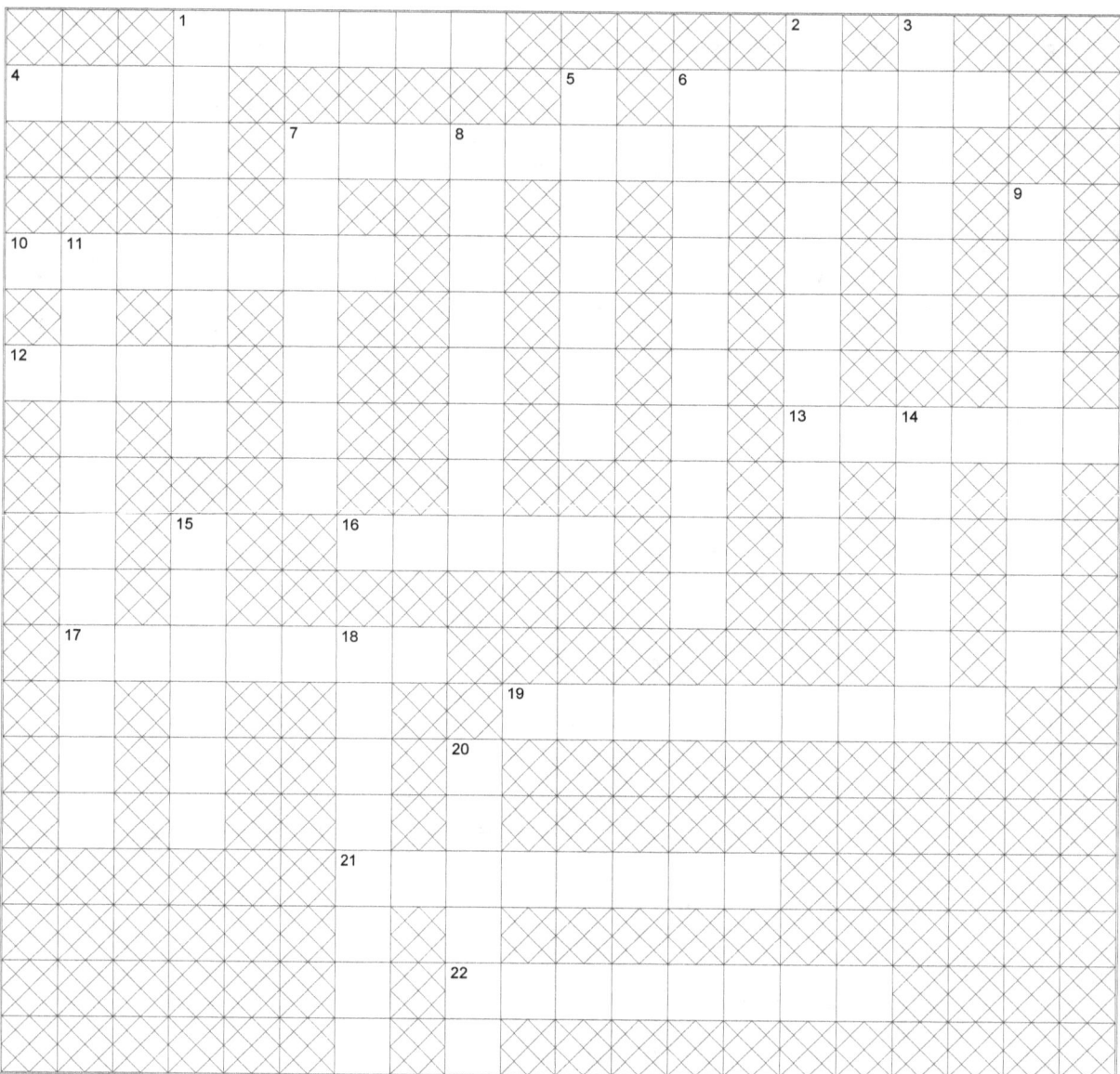

Across
1. To adhere, cling or stick fast
4. A chill or fit of shivering
6. To free from impurities
7. To punish
10. To pass (time) pleasantly
12. To consider
13. Special honor expressed publicly
16. To wait
17. To bring peace
19. Drunken merrymaking
21. Easily perceived
22. Of or relating to the body

Down
1. Harsh criticisms
2. To wave or flourish
3. Quickly and skillfully
5. Mask
6. Evil; wicked
7. A large vessel
8. Induced to commit an unlawful act
9. Steadfast adherence to a strict moral code
11. To avoid making an explicit statement
14. An obsequious follower
15. To fill with dismay
18. To hesitate as a result of conscience
20. Extreme ill will or spite

Macbeth Vocabulary Crossword 4 Answer Key

Across
1. To adhere, cling or stick fast
4. A chill or fit of shivering
6. To free from impurities
7. To punish
10. To pass (time) pleasantly
12. To consider
13. Special honor expressed publicly
16. To wait
17. To bring peace
19. Drunken merrymaking
21. Easily perceived
22. Of or relating to the body

Down
1. Harsh criticisms
2. To wave or flourish
3. Quickly and skillfully
5. Mask
6. Evil; wicked
7. A large vessel
8. Induced to commit an unlawful act
9. Steadfast adherence to a strict moral code
11. To avoid making an explicit statement
14. An obsequious follower
15. To fill with dismay
18. To hesitate as a result of conscience
20. Extreme ill will or spite

Macbeth Vocabulary Juggle Letters 1

1. CIIUOSREPN = 1. _____
   Evil; wicked

2. RVISDAZ = 2. _____
   Mask

3. EUNSRDOB = 3. _____
   Induced to commit an unlawful act

4. ERICIRPDA = 4. _____
   The murdering of one's father, mother or relative

5. LEBGEUI = 5. _____
   To pass (time) pleasantly

6. HDNREBDIAS = 6. _____
   To wave or flourish

7. HEAOMG = 7. _____
   Special honor expressed publicly

8. NOINIM = 8. _____
   An obsequious follower

9. AALBPLPE = 9. _____
   Easily perceived

10. UESM = 10. _____
    To consider

11. NRLCAOD = 11. _____
    A large vessel

12. DRGPUE = 12. _____
    To free from impurities

13. TNODNEICITIR = 13. _____
    To forbid authoritatively

14. APPLLA = 14. _____
    To fill with dismay

15. PRLCOORA = 15. _____
    Of or relating to the body

Macbeth Vocabulary Juggle Letters 1 Answer Key

1. CIIUOSREPN = 1. PERNICIOUS
   Evil; wicked

2. RVISDAZ = 2. VIZARDS
   Mask

3. EUNSRDOB = 3. SUBORNED
   Induced to commit an unlawful act

4. ERICIRPDA = 4. PARRICIDE
   The murdering of one's father, mother or relative

5. LEBGEUI = 5. BEGUILE
   To pass (time) pleasantly

6. HDNREBDIAS = 6. BRANDISHED
   To wave or flourish

7. HEAOMG = 7. HOMAGE
   Special honor expressed publicly

8. NOINIM = 8. MINION
   An obsequious follower

9. AALBPLPE = 9. PALPABLE
   Easily perceived

10. UESM = 10. MUSE
    To consider

11. NRLCAOD = 11. CALDRON
    A large vessel

12. DRGPUE = 12. PURGED
    To free from impurities

13. TNODNEICITIR = 13. INTERDICTION
    To forbid authoritatively

14. APPLLA = 14. APPALL
    To fill with dismay

15. PRLCOORA = 15. CORPORAL
    Of or relating to the body

Copyrighted

Macbeth Vocabulary Juggle Letters 2

1. OESCURRI = 1. _____
   A messenger

2. NRICDIETTOIN = 2. _____
   To forbid authoritatively

3. SEUM = 3. _____
   To consider

4. IALMCE = 4. _____
   Extreme ill will or spite

5. UIOTQSCAEVE = 5. _____
   To avoid making an explicit statement

6. UDGPER = 6. _____
   To free from impurities

7. UAGE = 7. _____
   A chill or fit of shivering

8. CSSEPRUL = 8. _____
   To hesitate as a result of conscience

9. SSEENRCU = 9. _____
   Harsh criticisms

10. NHEAISRDBD = 10. _____
    To wave or flourish

11. ROSCIAAUIV = 11. _____
    Immoderate desire for wealth

12. GILEBUE = 12. _____
    To pass (time) pleasantly

13. INAGROCSU = 13. _____
    Drunken merrymaking

14. ECEVAL = 14. _____
    To adhere, cling or stick fast

15. TNIGYITER = 15. _____
    Steadfast adherence to a strict moral code

Macbeth Vocabulary Juggle Letters 2 Answer Key

1. OESCURRI = 1. COURIERS
   A messenger

2. NRICDIETTOIN = 2. INTERDICTION
   To forbid authoritatively

3. SEUM = 3. MUSE
   To consider

4. IALMCE = 4. MALICE
   Extreme ill will or spite

5. UIOTQSCAEVE = 5. EQUIVOCATES
   To avoid making an explicit statement

6. UDGPER = 6. PURGED
   To free from impurities

7. UAGE = 7. AGUE
   A chill or fit of shivering

8. CSSEPRUL = 8. SCRUPLES
   To hesitate as a result of conscience

9. SSEENRCU = 9. CENSURES
   Harsh criticisms

10. NHEAISRDBD = 10. BRANDISHED
    To wave or flourish

11. ROSCIAAUIV = 11. AVARICIOUS
    Immoderate desire for wealth

12. GILEBUE = 12. BEGUILE
    To pass (time) pleasantly

13. INAGROCSU = 13. CAROUSING
    Drunken merrymaking

14. ECEVAL = 14. CLEAVE
    To adhere, cling or stick fast

15. TNIGYITER = 15. INTEGRITY
    Steadfast adherence to a strict moral code

Macbeth Vocabulary Juggle Letters 3

1. HACSTEIS = 1. _____
   To punish

2. EGPRDU = 2. _____
   To free from impurities

3. IEITMNUVID = 3. _____
   Extremely small in size

4. UGAE = 4. _____
   A chill or fit of shivering

5. DIBSE = 5. _____
   To wait

6. AGERNBIHR = 6. _____
   One that indicates what is to come

7. CESLPRUS = 7. _____
   To hesitate as a result of conscience

8. HSAIRBNEDD = 8. _____
   To wave or flourish

9. BLPLAPEA = 9. _____
   Easily perceived

10. AIIRUVAOCS =10. _____
    Immoderate desire for wealth

11. CIAMLE =11. _____
    Extreme ill will or spite

12. YTDFLE =12. _____
    Quickly and skillfully

13. NETIYIRGT =13. _____
    Steadfast adherence to a strict moral code

14. EEAAPPS =14. _____
    To bring peace

15. SERNSCEU =15. _____
    Harsh criticisms

Macbeth Vocabulary Juggle Letters 3 Answer Key

1. HACSTEIS = 1. CHASTISE
   To punish

2. EGPRDU = 2. PURGED
   To free from impurities

3. IEITMNUVID = 3. DIMINUTIVE
   Extremely small in size

4. UGAE = 4. AGUE
   A chill or fit of shivering

5. DIBSE = 5. BIDES
   To wait

6. AGERNBIHR = 6. HARBINGER
   One that indicates what is to come

7. CESLPRUS = 7. SCRUPLES
   To hesitate as a result of conscience

8. HSAIRBNEDD = 8. BRANDISHED
   To wave or flourish

9. BLPLAPEA = 9. PALPABLE
   Easily perceived

10. AIIRUVAOCS = 10. AVARICIOUS
    Immoderate desire for wealth

11. CIAMLE = 11. MALICE
    Extreme ill will or spite

12. YTDFLE = 12. DEFTLY
    Quickly and skillfully

13. NETIYIRGT = 13. INTEGRITY
    Steadfast adherence to a strict moral code

14. EEAAPPS = 14. APPEASE
    To bring peace

15. SERNSCEU = 15. CENSURES
    Harsh criticisms

Macbeth Vocabulary Juggle Letters 4

1. ONDLACR = 1. _____
   A large vessel

2. IMNINO = 2. _____
   An obsequious follower

3. EUGDRP = 3. _____
   To free from impurities

4. UERIORCS = 4. _____
   A messenger

5. TNGIIYTRE = 5. _____
   Steadfast adherence to a strict moral code

6. ACAUOIISRV = 6. _____
   Immoderate desire for wealth

7. AUGE = 7. _____
   A chill or fit of shivering

8. RBNHIGARE = 8. _____
   One that indicates what is to come

9. CEIQTSEOAUV = 9. _____
   To avoid making an explicit statement

10. DSIBE = 10. _____
    To wait

11. LEDYTF = 11. _____
    Quickly and skillfully

12. SOEPINIRUC = 12. _____
    Evil; wicked

13. VCEAEL = 13. _____
    To adhere, cling or stick fast

14. DROUBESN = 14. _____
    Induced to commit an unlawful act

15. AHOMGE = 15. _____
    Special honor expressed publicly

Macbeth Vocabulary Juggle Letters 4 Answer Key

1. ONDLACR = 1. CALDRON
   A large vessel

2. IMNINO = 2. MINION
   An obsequious follower

3. EUGDRP = 3. PURGED
   To free from impurities

4. UERIORCS = 4. COURIERS
   A messenger

5. TNGIIYTRE = 5. INTEGRITY
   Steadfast adherence to a strict moral code

6. ACAUOIISRV = 6. AVARICIOUS
   Immoderate desire for wealth

7. AUGE = 7. AGUE
   A chill or fit of shivering

8. RBNHIGARE = 8. HARBINGER
   One that indicates what is to come

9. CEIQTSEOAUV = 9. EQUIVOCATES
   To avoid making an explicit statement

10. DSIBE =10. BIDES
    To wait

11. LEDYTF =11. DEFTLY
    Quickly and skillfully

12. SOEPINIRUC =12. PERNICIOUS
    Evil; wicked

13. VCEAEL =13. CLEAVE
    To adhere, cling or stick fast

14. DROUBESN =14. SUBORNED
    Induced to commit an unlawful act

15. AHOMGE =15. HOMAGE
    Special honor expressed publicly

AGUE	A chill or fit of shivering
APPALL	To fill with dismay
APPEASE	To bring peace
AVARICIOUS	Immoderate desire for wealth
BEGUILE	To pass (time) pleasantly
BIDES	To wait

BRANDISHED	To wave or flourish
CALDRON	A large vessel
CAROUSING	Drunken merrymaking
CENSURES	Harsh criticisms
CHASTISE	To punish
CLEAVE	To adhere, cling or stick fast

CORPORAL	Of or relating to the body
COURIERS	A messenger
DEFTLY	Quickly and skillfully
DIMINUTIVE	Extremely small in size
EQUIVOCATES	To avoid making an explicit statement
HARBINGER	One that indicates what is to come

HOMAGE	Special honor expressed publicly
INTEGRITY	Steadfast adherence to a strict moral code
INTERDICTION	To forbid authoritatively
MALICE	Extreme ill will or spite
MINION	An obsequious follower
MUSE	To consider

PALPABLE	Easily perceived
PARRICIDE	The murdering of one's father, mother or relative
PERNICIOUS	Evil; wicked
PURGED	To free from impurities
SCRUPLES	To hesitate as a result of conscience
SUBORNED	Induced to commit an unlawful act

VIZARDS	Mask

Macbeth Vocabulary

INTEGRITY	MALICE	DIMINUTIVE	COURIERS	MUSE
AGUE	HARBINGER	CAROUSING	BRANDISHED	BEGUILE
CLEAVE	PURGED	FREE SPACE	CHASTISE	SUBORNED
BIDES	HOMAGE	VIZARDS	CENSURES	SCRUPLES
APPALL	PERNICIOUS	CORPORAL	PALPABLE	AVARICIOUS

Macbeth Vocabulary

EQUIVOCATES	PARRICIDE	MINION	APPEASE	INTERDICTION
DEFTLY	AVARICIOUS	PALPABLE	CORPORAL	PERNICIOUS
APPALL	SCRUPLES	FREE SPACE	VIZARDS	HOMAGE
BIDES	SUBORNED	CHASTISE	CALDRON	PURGED
CLEAVE	BEGUILE	BRANDISHED	CAROUSING	HARBINGER

Macbeth Vocabulary

CHASTISE	PERNICIOUS	INTEGRITY	APPALL	AVARICIOUS
INTERDICTION	BIDES	APPEASE	CALDRON	SUBORNED
MINION	CAROUSING	FREE SPACE	MALICE	COURIERS
EQUIVOCATES	CENSURES	CLEAVE	MUSE	DIMINUTIVE
HARBINGER	HOMAGE	VIZARDS	CORPORAL	PARRICIDE

Macbeth Vocabulary

DEFTLY	BRANDISHED	SCRUPLES	PALPABLE	AGUE
BEGUILE	PARRICIDE	CORPORAL	VIZARDS	HOMAGE
HARBINGER	DIMINUTIVE	FREE SPACE	CLEAVE	CENSURES
EQUIVOCATES	COURIERS	MALICE	PURGED	CAROUSING
MINION	SUBORNED	CALDRON	APPEASE	BIDES

Macbeth Vocabulary

HOMAGE	INTERDICTION	APPEASE	CENSURES	CORPORAL
CLEAVE	APPALL	CALDRON	VIZARDS	HARBINGER
PURGED	EQUIVOCATES	FREE SPACE	MUSE	BRANDISHED
AVARICIOUS	BEGUILE	COURIERS	AGUE	SUBORNED
PARRICIDE	PERNICIOUS	CHASTISE	MALICE	PALPABLE

Macbeth Vocabulary

BIDES	DIMINUTIVE	DEFTLY	MINION	CAROUSING
INTEGRITY	PALPABLE	MALICE	CHASTISE	PERNICIOUS
PARRICIDE	SUBORNED	FREE SPACE	COURIERS	BEGUILE
AVARICIOUS	BRANDISHED	MUSE	SCRUPLES	EQUIVOCATES
PURGED	HARBINGER	VIZARDS	CALDRON	APPALL

Macbeth Vocabulary

INTERDICTION	HARBINGER	MUSE	CAROUSING	CENSURES
DIMINUTIVE	HOMAGE	EQUIVOCATES	PARRICIDE	PERNICIOUS
PALPABLE	SUBORNED	FREE SPACE	APPALL	CHASTISE
VIZARDS	COURIERS	AGUE	CORPORAL	CLEAVE
CALDRON	MINION	PURGED	AVARICIOUS	SCRUPLES

Macbeth Vocabulary

BEGUILE	DEFTLY	BRANDISHED	INTEGRITY	BIDES
MALICE	SCRUPLES	AVARICIOUS	PURGED	MINION
CALDRON	CLEAVE	FREE SPACE	AGUE	COURIERS
VIZARDS	CHASTISE	APPALL	APPEASE	SUBORNED
PALPABLE	PERNICIOUS	PARRICIDE	EQUIVOCATES	HOMAGE

Macbeth Vocabulary

CHASTISE	DEFTLY	AGUE	VIZARDS	HARBINGER
APPEASE	BIDES	CLEAVE	PARRICIDE	AVARICIOUS
COURIERS	INTEGRITY	FREE SPACE	MUSE	MINION
CORPORAL	MALICE	PERNICIOUS	SUBORNED	HOMAGE
APPALL	PALPABLE	CAROUSING	BEGUILE	DIMINUTIVE

Macbeth Vocabulary

CENSURES	EQUIVOCATES	CALDRON	SCRUPLES	BRANDISHED
INTERDICTION	DIMINUTIVE	BEGUILE	CAROUSING	PALPABLE
APPALL	HOMAGE	FREE SPACE	PERNICIOUS	MALICE
CORPORAL	MINION	MUSE	PURGED	INTEGRITY
COURIERS	AVARICIOUS	PARRICIDE	CLEAVE	BIDES

Macbeth Vocabulary

SUBORNED	DIMINUTIVE	BIDES	HOMAGE	CALDRON
CENSURES	SCRUPLES	MUSE	EQUIVOCATES	PURGED
CAROUSING	BRANDISHED	FREE SPACE	CLEAVE	MINION
APPALL	PARRICIDE	PERNICIOUS	COURIERS	CORPORAL
AVARICIOUS	INTEGRITY	MALICE	INTERDICTION	CHASTISE

Macbeth Vocabulary

PALPABLE	APPEASE	DEFTLY	AGUE	BEGUILE
HARBINGER	CHASTISE	INTERDICTION	MALICE	INTEGRITY
AVARICIOUS	CORPORAL	FREE SPACE	PERNICIOUS	PARRICIDE
APPALL	MINION	CLEAVE	VIZARDS	BRANDISHED
CAROUSING	PURGED	EQUIVOCATES	MUSE	SCRUPLES

Macbeth Vocabulary

HARBINGER	DEFTLY	HOMAGE	DIMINUTIVE	PALPABLE
SCRUPLES	CAROUSING	PURGED	AVARICIOUS	BRANDISHED
PERNICIOUS	CALDRON	FREE SPACE	COURIERS	CLEAVE
VIZARDS	MUSE	SUBORNED	INTEGRITY	CENSURES
CORPORAL	PARRICIDE	BEGUILE	APPALL	MALICE

Macbeth Vocabulary

APPEASE	BIDES	CHASTISE	AGUE	MINION
INTERDICTION	MALICE	APPALL	BEGUILE	PARRICIDE
CORPORAL	CENSURES	FREE SPACE	SUBORNED	MUSE
VIZARDS	CLEAVE	COURIERS	EQUIVOCATES	CALDRON
PERNICIOUS	BRANDISHED	AVARICIOUS	PURGED	CAROUSING

Macbeth Vocabulary

COURIERS	CENSURES	MINION	APPEASE	SUBORNED
PURGED	EQUIVOCATES	HARBINGER	CORPORAL	VIZARDS
CAROUSING	CHASTISE	FREE SPACE	MALICE	APPALL
PERNICIOUS	CLEAVE	PARRICIDE	BEGUILE	BRANDISHED
DIMINUTIVE	PALPABLE	MUSE	HOMAGE	SCRUPLES

Macbeth Vocabulary

AVARICIOUS	CALDRON	INTEGRITY	AGUE	DEFTLY
INTERDICTION	SCRUPLES	HOMAGE	MUSE	PALPABLE
DIMINUTIVE	BRANDISHED	FREE SPACE	PARRICIDE	CLEAVE
PERNICIOUS	APPALL	MALICE	BIDES	CHASTISE
CAROUSING	VIZARDS	CORPORAL	HARBINGER	EQUIVOCATES

Macbeth Vocabulary

CALDRON	PERNICIOUS	DIMINUTIVE	CAROUSING	INTERDICTION
BIDES	HOMAGE	COURIERS	APPEASE	CENSURES
CHASTISE	DEFTLY	FREE SPACE	INTEGRITY	CLEAVE
MALICE	SUBORNED	BEGUILE	EQUIVOCATES	PURGED
CORPORAL	SCRUPLES	PALPABLE	MINION	PARRICIDE

Macbeth Vocabulary

BRANDISHED	VIZARDS	AGUE	APPALL	HARBINGER
MUSE	PARRICIDE	MINION	PALPABLE	SCRUPLES
CORPORAL	PURGED	FREE SPACE	BEGUILE	SUBORNED
MALICE	CLEAVE	INTEGRITY	AVARICIOUS	DEFTLY
CHASTISE	CENSURES	APPEASE	COURIERS	HOMAGE

Macbeth Vocabulary

HARBINGER	BIDES	MUSE	APPEASE	PARRICIDE
HOMAGE	PERNICIOUS	SUBORNED	CLEAVE	AGUE
INTERDICTION	INTEGRITY	FREE SPACE	MALICE	DIMINUTIVE
CORPORAL	CALDRON	VIZARDS	CAROUSING	APPALL
DEFTLY	SCRUPLES	CHASTISE	MINION	COURIERS

Macbeth Vocabulary

PALPABLE	AVARICIOUS	BEGUILE	BRANDISHED	CENSURES
EQUIVOCATES	COURIERS	MINION	CHASTISE	SCRUPLES
DEFTLY	APPALL	FREE SPACE	VIZARDS	CALDRON
CORPORAL	DIMINUTIVE	MALICE	PURGED	INTEGRITY
INTERDICTION	AGUE	CLEAVE	SUBORNED	PERNICIOUS

Macbeth Vocabulary

APPEASE	BIDES	PARRICIDE	CENSURES	INTEGRITY
AVARICIOUS	CORPORAL	COURIERS	MALICE	SCRUPLES
PURGED	EQUIVOCATES	FREE SPACE	MINION	AGUE
DEFTLY	CHASTISE	BEGUILE	INTERDICTION	MUSE
CLEAVE	VIZARDS	HOMAGE	DIMINUTIVE	APPALL

Macbeth Vocabulary

SUBORNED	BRANDISHED	PALPABLE	HARBINGER	CALDRON
CAROUSING	APPALL	DIMINUTIVE	HOMAGE	VIZARDS
CLEAVE	MUSE	FREE SPACE	BEGUILE	CHASTISE
DEFTLY	AGUE	MINION	PERNICIOUS	EQUIVOCATES
PURGED	SCRUPLES	MALICE	COURIERS	CORPORAL

Macbeth Vocabulary

BEGUILE	HARBINGER	PARRICIDE	APPALL	MUSE
DIMINUTIVE	CHASTISE	CALDRON	BRANDISHED	APPEASE
AGUE	MINION	FREE SPACE	PERNICIOUS	VIZARDS
BIDES	MALICE	CAROUSING	SCRUPLES	DEFTLY
CLEAVE	SUBORNED	INTERDICTION	PALPABLE	INTEGRITY

Macbeth Vocabulary

COURIERS	EQUIVOCATES	CENSURES	PURGED	CORPORAL
HOMAGE	INTEGRITY	PALPABLE	INTERDICTION	SUBORNED
CLEAVE	DEFTLY	FREE SPACE	CAROUSING	MALICE
BIDES	VIZARDS	PERNICIOUS	AVARICIOUS	MINION
AGUE	APPEASE	BRANDISHED	CALDRON	CHASTISE

Macbeth Vocabulary

CALDRON	CENSURES	HOMAGE	MUSE	PERNICIOUS
VIZARDS	EQUIVOCATES	SUBORNED	CAROUSING	BEGUILE
CHASTISE	PARRICIDE	FREE SPACE	PURGED	BRANDISHED
AGUE	CLEAVE	BIDES	MALICE	INTERDICTION
INTEGRITY	APPEASE	DIMINUTIVE	APPALL	SCRUPLES

Macbeth Vocabulary

HARBINGER	PALPABLE	COURIERS	MINION	CORPORAL
AVARICIOUS	SCRUPLES	APPALL	DIMINUTIVE	APPEASE
INTEGRITY	INTERDICTION	FREE SPACE	BIDES	CLEAVE
AGUE	BRANDISHED	PURGED	DEFTLY	PARRICIDE
CHASTISE	BEGUILE	CAROUSING	SUBORNED	EQUIVOCATES

Macbeth Vocabulary

APPEASE	CLEAVE	SUBORNED	MALICE	HOMAGE
PERNICIOUS	VIZARDS	CORPORAL	AGUE	INTEGRITY
BEGUILE	INTERDICTION	FREE SPACE	DEFTLY	CAROUSING
BIDES	MUSE	CALDRON	CENSURES	PALPABLE
APPALL	AVARICIOUS	BRANDISHED	PURGED	CHASTISE

Macbeth Vocabulary

EQUIVOCATES	COURIERS	HARBINGER	SCRUPLES	PARRICIDE
MINION	CHASTISE	PURGED	BRANDISHED	AVARICIOUS
APPALL	PALPABLE	FREE SPACE	CALDRON	MUSE
BIDES	CAROUSING	DEFTLY	DIMINUTIVE	INTERDICTION
BEGUILE	INTEGRITY	AGUE	CORPORAL	VIZARDS

Macbeth Vocabulary

PERNICIOUS	HARBINGER	APPALL	MALICE	AGUE
SCRUPLES	BEGUILE	DEFTLY	MUSE	MINION
AVARICIOUS	CENSURES	FREE SPACE	BRANDISHED	BIDES
CLEAVE	VIZARDS	CORPORAL	APPEASE	EQUIVOCATES
CALDRON	CHASTISE	PURGED	CAROUSING	PALPABLE

Macbeth Vocabulary

PARRICIDE	INTERDICTION	INTEGRITY	DIMINUTIVE	HOMAGE
SUBORNED	PALPABLE	CAROUSING	PURGED	CHASTISE
CALDRON	EQUIVOCATES	FREE SPACE	CORPORAL	VIZARDS
CLEAVE	BIDES	BRANDISHED	COURIERS	CENSURES
AVARICIOUS	MINION	MUSE	DEFTLY	BEGUILE

Macbeth Vocabulary

DIMINUTIVE	APPALL	PALPABLE	MUSE	PERNICIOUS
DEFTLY	CAROUSING	BEGUILE	VIZARDS	CLEAVE
HOMAGE	PURGED	FREE SPACE	MINION	AGUE
CORPORAL	PARRICIDE	COURIERS	INTERDICTION	CHASTISE
BRANDISHED	CALDRON	BIDES	APPEASE	AVARICIOUS

Macbeth Vocabulary

MALICE	INTEGRITY	HARBINGER	SCRUPLES	SUBORNED
EQUIVOCATES	AVARICIOUS	APPEASE	BIDES	CALDRON
BRANDISHED	CHASTISE	FREE SPACE	COURIERS	PARRICIDE
CORPORAL	AGUE	MINION	CENSURES	PURGED
HOMAGE	CLEAVE	VIZARDS	BEGUILE	CAROUSING